Wincheap Memories

Robert Brett & Sons' depot and sports ground at Wincheap, Canterbury, on a weekday afternoon in late summer, *circa* 1952. In the foreground, an East Kent double-decker pulls away from the bus stop at the junction of Thanington Road and Cockering Road and passes the carefully-tended Thanington Allotment Gardens. A hearse prepares to overtake the bus, and a van is about to turn into the depot's 'top yard.' The yard and the garage alongside it are almost deserted but in a few hours Bretts' drivers will return from their day's work and the yard will be busy with gravel lorries manoeuvring into their overnight parking spaces. Beyond the commercial site, at the football ground known as 'Bretts' Corner', the grandstand and terraces are ready to receive supporters of Canterbury City FC and the club's Kent League opponents. Bill Longley, the company's groundsman, has prepared the pitch for the first home match; soon he will fence-off the cricket square and place duckboards around the perimeter of the pitch, to protect the greensward from the trampling feet of fans who prefer to watch from the sidelines. A poplar tree planted by Robert Brett in 1935 casts its shadow towards the corner of the penalty area at the Thanington end. Behind the goals, traces of an old cinder cycling and athletics circuit are revealed in the sunbaked turf, as if for an airborne archaeologist. A tranquil scene, remarkable for the almost complete absence of traffic and people. *(Skyfotos/Fotoflite/ Malcolm Longley collection)*

Wincheap Memories

A pictorial history
of a corner of Canterbury

Paul Tritton

Brett

First published 1996

ISBN 0 9527789 0 4

Robert Brett & Sons Limited
Robert Brett House
Milton Manor Farm
Ashford Road
Canterbury
Kent CT4 7PP
Telephone 01227/829000 Fax 01227/762601

Printed by the KPC Group, Ashford, Kent TN24 OBP

British Library Cataloguing in Publication Data
A catalogue record for this book is available from the British Library

Employees of Robert Brett & Sons gather around an East Kent coach at the entrance to 'carpenters' yard', Wincheap Depot, before an outing to London in 1948. Personnel identified are (from the left), standing: (1) Bert Killian, (2) Bill Gipps, (3) Albert Weatherall, (4) George Knight, (5) Bert Sackett, (6) George Weatherall, (8) George West, (9) Bill Stone, (10) Sam Brown, (11) Ray Marsh, (12) Dick Fedarb, (14) Fred Marsh, (15) Fred Jones; front row: (1) Fred Sharp, (2) Percy Sackett, (3) Horace Weatherall, (4) Jimmy Hawkins.

Contents

Acknowledgements

My grateful thanks to the Brett family; to the directors of Robert Brett & Sons Limited; and to the many past, present and retired employees of the company (and relatives of employees) who supplied photographs and information, and patiently answered my many questions while I was producing this book.

Special thanks to my wife Patricia; to my parents, Ted and Mary Tritton; to my in-laws, Percy and Dorothy Sackett; and to David Elliott, Tim Keenan and Nigel Tilly.

I am also indebted to the staffs of the Centre for Kentish Studies, Canterbury Cathedral Archives, Canterbury Reference Library and Local Studies Department, Kent County Council Records Centre, and Canterbury Museums and Galleries; and to Sara Bailey, Bob Bounds and Dianne Stingemore (Kentish Gazette, Canterbury); Jim Beale; Alan Bensted; Tony Blake; Jo Burn (BBC Radio Kent); Derek Butler; Iain Cameron; Dennis Cavie, Bernard Chittenden; Derek Collyer; Paul Crampton; Harold Daniels; Bill Datlen; Pat and Sheila Entwistle; Lynne Ewart; David France; Audrey Gant; Ron Gant; Norman Greensted; John Hambrook; Frank Hammersley; David Hay (Group Archivist, British Telecom); Rev. Tim Herbert; E.A. Hopewell; Barry Hollis (Kent Messenger); Terry Hougham; Lilian Inge; Doug Inkpen; Frank Jones; R.F. Jones; Michael R. Lane, Peter Legg and Bob Whitehead (Road Locomotive Society); Chris Laming (Lyons Funeral Service); Glyn Lee (Charles Burrell Museum); Jean Lynes; David Manners; Cyril May; John Maxwell (Mowll & Mowll); Tina Newport; Charles Parry; John Parsons; Jack Pilbeam; Reeves & Neylan; Marion Rigden; Bob Simmonds; Pamela Slade; Keith Smith; David Swain; Bernard Thomas; Christopher Wacher (Furley Page Fielding & Barton); Phyllis Wellard; Gerry Whittaker; William Worrell; Arthur Wright.

Unless otherwise credited, all photographs are from collections owned by Robert Brett & Sons Limited or by members of the Brett family. I am especially grateful to the Kent Messenger Group for kind permission to publish photographs from its newspapers, particularly the Kentish Gazette.

All reasonable efforts were made correctly to identify people and locations featured in the photographs. I will be pleased to hear from any readers able to correct, or add to, any of the information in the text.

Paul Tritton
May 1996

Introduction

IMAGINE that it is 1952 — give or take a year — and we are travelling to Wincheap on the top deck of a Guy Arab No. 27 East Kent bus. We caught the bus at the 'top of the town', opposite Canterbury cattle market; luckily, we found a front seat. Our conductor, Fred Cuckoo, is climbing the stairs, calling 'Any more fares?', and in compliance with the notice imploring us to TENDER EXACT FARE AND STATE DESTINATION we have our three ha'pence ready.

We turn into Wincheap Street at the corner of Station Road East, where the road dips under the London, Chatham and Dover Railway and climbs between raised, railed pavements. On our right a few passers-by are peering at the tiny black and white screens of the Ferranti television sets in the window of Southwood's electrical shop; next door, Mr Manklow, newsagent and tobacconist, is busy selling Daily Heralds, Eagles, Woodbines and anything else his customers care to read or smoke, while his friendly black Labrador sleeps in the shade cast by the shop window's canopy.

A moment ago, at the junction of Castle Street and Wincheap Street, we passed the head office of 'British Road Services (R.H.E.) Unit A.78' and now our driver, Bill Datlen, will probably give way to a lorry turning into BRS's depot in Tudor Road, to our left. We remember the office and depot as they were before nationalisation, when they belonged to Charles and George Yeoman, proprietors of one of four haulage firms whose steam and motor vehicles operated from premises in or just off Wincheap in days not long gone by.

We are travelling through a townscape that has hardly changed since the turn of the century. Between the two railway bridges — the first within sight of the city walls, the other on the Victorian outskirts of Canterbury — Wincheap still resembles the high street of a small country town, with busy shops and pubs and, among them, houses with worn but well-scrubbed front steps leading directly down to the pavement. It is a district that is self-sufficient in the basic necessities of life; almost everything we need from the cradle to the grave is here, including a midwife, Nurse Letitia Lynes, at No. 1 Greenfield Cottages, and an undertaker, H.A. Mitchell & Sons, at No. 137 Wincheap. All that seems to be lacking are some churches and chapels. St Andrew's Presbyterian Church at Wincheap Green is the nearest, but Anglicans have further to travel to their Place of Worship; part of Wincheap is in St Mildred's parish, whose church is within the city, close by the Norman Castle, while the rest of the district — including the western end, towards which we are heading — is in the parish of St Nicholas, whose church is in Thanington.

As we continue our journey we glance up the many side-streets, such as Victoria Road, and see the homes of generations of citizens of all ranks and professions. No. 1 Victoria Road was the home of John William Farmery, a former Chief Constable of Canterbury City Police.

Just past the King's Head pub we come to the Wincheap Nonconformist Burial

Ground. Here lie about three hundred Canterbury dissenters, including Thomas Clark, whose tune Cranbrook became world-famous when chosen for the song On Ilkley Moor; and George Felix Finn, traction engine proprietor and athletics promoter.

G.F. Finn is by now an almost forgotten citizen but Finn & Co., the business he founded 70 years ago, still trades nearby in Seymour Place. His son, Felix George Finn, now nearly 80 years old, lives at No. 31 Gordon Road with his wife Louisa Frances. Gordon Road was the first turning we passed at the bottom of the street.

The burial ground is in the shadow of the Elham Valley Railway embankment, and we pass under the railway at the corners of Cow Lane and Hollow Lane. The street is now predominantly residential, with terraced cottages and detached and semi-detached houses extending nearly as far as the eye can see. One of the 'semis' is Culham, No. 91 Wincheap. This was Herbert and Winifred Brett's home in the 1920s, during the first few years of their marriage. Bert was the youngest of the four sons of Robert Brett, founder of Robert Brett & Sons, haulage contractors and quarry owners.

The houses hereabouts have small front gardens but soon we are at Thanington Cottages, with only a pavement between their front doors and Wincheap's infrequent traffic (we are making our journey in the 1950s, remember). The first cottage, Prospect House, No. 96 Wincheap, was Robert and Emma Brett's home at the time Robert set up his business.

When Robert was one of G.F. Finn's engine drivers, he and Emma lived at No. 4 Thanington Cottages, at the other end of the terrace. They had a large family — four boys and three girls. We can see that the cottage is little more than a 'two up, two down', with an attic bedroom that was probably shared by the daughters. The Bretts moved to Prospect House, a much larger property than its neighbours, in 1908, soon after the birth of their youngest child, Grace.

The next row of cottages is Marlowe Terrace. G.F. Finn and his family lived at No. 1. Between here and No. 4 Thanington Cottages we can peep over a high wall which has three bricked-up openings and a pair of very solid gates. The pavement in front of the gates is cobbled and slopes down to the street, forming a 'run in' for vehicles.

Inside the gates there are a few timber and corrugated iron buildings, once part of Mr Finn's Thanington Engineering Works. They are grouped around a small yard where, 50 years ago, one or two traction engines would be parked, waiting to be repaired in time for their next haulage contract.

At the far end of Marlowe Terrace stands the Hop Poles pub, so named because there are hop gardens just across the way. The pub was rebuilt in 1904, when its immediate neighbours were William Lillywhite's oast house (which we can see above the rooftops) and Thanington Dairy, owned by J. Smith, whose son Frank married Robert and Emma's eldest daughter, Elizabeth. The premises are now occupied by the Apollinaris Company, mineral water manufacturers.

Close by, down a flight of steps, are Waterworks Cottages, in the shadow of an enormous tree, beyond which are two more pairs of gates. These are the entrances to 'top yard' — part of Wincheap Depot, home of Robert Brett & Sons' transport fleet, workshops and precision engineering factory. Through the gates we may see some tipper lorries bearing the name 'Bretts Quarries' parked in front of a long garage, but between the gates there is a tall hoarding and even from the top of our bus we will only just be able to see over it. Entirely beyond our view are 'bottom yard', where vehicles and heavy machinery are constantly passing through the high and wide entrances into the workshops and factory, and an area still called 'the orchard', which has become a compound for lorries and mobile plant waiting to be repaired.

Wincheap Street ends at 'top yard' and we must alight at the next stop. We are one mile from the centre of Canterbury. Ahead, the main road follows the Stour valley to Ashford, while to our left Cockering Road climbs gently to Chartham Downs. If we cross over to the corner of 'top yard' a lane will lead us to Bretts' Sports Ground, where we can watch a game of cricket or join in the chorus of 'Set 'em alight, City' at one of Canterbury City Football Club's home matches.

We have reached the end of our journey — and the beginning of our story.

An era of change and redevelopment that lasted for more than 40 years began in Wincheap in 1955, when the Elham Valley Railway bridge was dismantled, followed by the creation of a trading estate off Cow Lane. In 1963 the construction of a roundabout and dual carriageway for the Canterbury ring road completely transformed the city end of Wincheap Street; several fine houses, a pub and some cottages had to be demolished to make way for the new road. In 1966, at the Thanington end of the street, Robert Brett & Sons opened a new head office, Brett House, on the site of the big garage at Wincheap Depot. In October 1981 the A2 Canterbury by-pass was opened, concluding a civil engineering programme which involved building a bridge and a new junction where Wincheap, Cockering Road and Thanington Road converge. In October 1994 the Wincheap Park and Ride Service started operating from a car park and bus terminus built on the western edge of Bretts' Sports Ground, and on what had been Thanington Allotment Gardens.

On September 4, 1995, Safeway Stores began to redevelop Wincheap Depot and the sports ground, and before long completed one of the biggest changes in Wincheap in living memory.

This book commemorates 113 years of work and recreation at the place where G.F. Finn and Robert Brett & Sons contributed so much to Canterbury's business and social life. It is a remarkable story, just one of its many fascinating aspects being that the Brett family had an unbroken link with the place for 112 of those years: from 1884, when Robert Brett helped George Finn create the sports ground, to March 1996, when Robert's grandsons Tim and Tony and great-grandsons Stephen and Bill and their staff said goodbye to Brett House and moved to new headquarters a mile and a half to the west, at Milton Manor Farm.

Most of the photographs in this collection were taken at Finn and Bretts' premises in Wincheap, but we have not forgotten the employees who reported for work there every morning and then spent the rest of the day driving traction engines and lorries, operating Bretts' construction machinery, and maintaining the firm's plant and equipment all over east Kent. Memories of their working lives extend beyond

Wincheap and they are seen at places some distance from their base, and at functions where they joined colleagues from Bretts' other departments in and around Canterbury.

The Wincheap site was known by several names. Those who worked in the complex of workshops and garages beside and beyond 'top yard' remember their days at 'Wincheap Depot' or 'the yard'; office workers knew the place as 'head office'; engineers talk of having worked at 'CPE', the precision engineering factory which occupied part of the premises for about 45 years. To sports enthusiasts, what went on beyond the commercial site was much more important; they look back to happy hours at 'Bretts' Corner', the name given to Bretts' Sports Ground when Kent League football was played there.

Perhaps 'Bretts' Corner' will be the name that will endure for this affectionately remembered corner of Canterbury, even though it is shoppers, not soccer fans, who gather there in their hundreds today.

Xmas 1911

Mr Brett

Dr. to **J. SMITH,**

Thanington Dairy,

CANTERBURY, KENT.

To 2 Truck Load manure		1-12-0
To 4 Barrow Load		1-0
	£	1.13.0

Paid J Smith

Dec 29th 1911

1: Green shoots

A sports meeting, fête and military tournament at the County Athletic Grounds, Wincheap, during the late Victorian or Edwardian period. A crowd has gathered around the perimeter of the cycling and running track to watch an Army display. Lillywhite's oast house (today occupied by 'Pine & Things') is behind the roundabout. The roofs of Thanington Cottages and other houses in Wincheap fill the skyline beyond the other sideshows.

WINCHEAP Depot and Bretts' Sports Ground were developed on a 9.5 acre field which, together with an adjacent smaller field extending to the River Stour, belonged to the Sankey family for about 150 years. In 1888 Herbert Tritton Sankey sold the land to John E. Wiltshier. By then George Felix Finn was renting the larger of the fields and a group of buildings, called the Thanington Engineering Works, on its south-east boundary.

G.F. Finn (b. June 13, 1835) was the son of George Finn, housepainter, and Esther Finn of No. 3 St Peter's Place, Canterbury. In 1872 he went into business as a contractor, steam engineer and boiler maker at St Thomas's Engineering Co. in Whitstable Road, Canterbury, and bought three steam rollers built by Thomas Green & Co. of Leeds. He moved to Wincheap in the 1880s, expanding his engineering business and converting the field into the County Athletic Grounds. His first sports meeting, on Whit Tuesday, May 15, 1883, attracted about 14,000 spectators; 20 guineas of gate-money were donated to the Kent and Canterbury Hospital (then in Longport, Canterbury). His cinder cycling and running track, a quarter of a mile in circumference, was praised as 'one of the finest in England.'

In 1884, when he was 16 years old, Robert Brett left his family's home at Pix Hill, Great Mongeham, near Deal, where his father, Stephen, was the bailiff at a 156-acre farm, and came to Canterbury to work for Mr Finn. One of his first jobs was to help plant a row of poplar trees on the edge of the sports ground. Later he became a traction engine driver. By now Mr Finn had bought several more steam road locomotives — including some Aveling & Porters, a Burrell, a Fowler and two McLarens. Over the years about 23 steam locos of various types and makes were bought for the Finn fleet. Until recently it was thought that only a few photographs of Finn's early locomotives — and only one of Robert Brett as an engine driver — existed. However, a collection of undated and in some cases damaged glass negatives of local views and events, taken by an unknown photographer, was discovered in December 1995; the collection included several pre-First World War pictures of Finn's vehicles at or near Wincheap Depot or at work in the countryside, and of events at his sports ground. Four of the photographs show Robert with one of Finn's Aveling & Porters (probably no. 2092, a 'high wheeler' single cylinder 8hp road engine built in 1885) and appear to have been taken on the same day. The discovery of the negatives coincided with the donation, to Robert Brett & Sons Ltd, of an ancient, badly damaged photograph that once belonged to the late Fred 'Topper' Foster of Barham and evidently was previously owned by J.W. Keeler, a builder in the village. The photograph matched one of the negatives, and bore a handwritten caption which revealed that it was taken in 1898 at Turks Hill, Covet Lane, Kingston.

For 30 years the County Athletic Grounds (also known as Wincheap Athletic Grounds, Finn's Ground and Pay's Ground at various times) was a venue for athletics, circuses, cycle races, fairs, fêtes, soccer matches between local club and Army teams, Whitsun holiday sports days, and cricket. 'Lord' George Sanger's circus came here in 1887 and 1902; Sir Robert Fossett's Circus in 1908. A sports day and fête on Whit Tuesday 1895 attracted a crowd of more than 6,000. W. F. Randall had announced that he would fly a Montgolfier balloon over the field and release a life-size figure on a parachute; unfortunately the balloon became entangled in a tree and caught fire. Later, 'Professor Gyl, the Cosmopolitan Wonder' demonstrated his 'Perpendicular Rope and Lightning Drop' without mishap.

The first proper flight at the sports ground was probably Professor Drake's 'majestic trip to the heavens' in a hot air balloon, and his 'very successful' descent by parachute. This took place on Whit Tuesday 1900, when the programme also included 'an exhibition of war balloons' and motor cycle racing. A.C. Arter drove the seven miles from his garage at Barham to the sports ground on his De Dion motor tricycle in 20 minutes, to take part in 'a race against time.' The cycle track's sharp bends slowed him down to just over 30 miles an hour, and a puncture forced him to abandon his demonstration after 20 laps.

G.F. Finn died on February 14, 1909. At about this time his business moved to Seymour Place, Wincheap, and was sold. It continued trading as Finn & Co., Engineers, and was run by Albert Vincent Allen and his son, Vincent. Reporting Mr Finn's funeral, the Kent Herald said: 'His repute as a handicapper was recognized throughout the county ... the world of sport has lost one of its most experienced and esteemed supporters ... having been a free thinker, there was no religious service at the graveside.' He was a Forester and a member of the Ancient Order of Druids and of the Grand Loyal and Philanthropic Order of Prussian Hermits.

According to Brett family tradition, Robert Brett 'laid the foundations of his business on February 7, 1904', five years before Mr Finn died. The Thanington Rate Books show that the engineering workshops and sports ground were vacant for a short time after Finn's firm moved to Seymour Place, and that Robert became their 'occupier' in April 1910. He seems to have had no interest in, or use for, the sports ground, which for the next few years was managed by A.J.Pay, who continued to promote sports events there. Mr Pay lived in Victoria Road and owned the Hop Poles pub.

Use of the sports ground declined from about 1913, although from then until about 1920 the Simon Langton Schools held their annual athletic sports there. During the Great War a military camp was set up in Thanington; an Army 'horse hospital' is said to have been located in part of the building that housed a sawmill on the edge of the sports ground. Many years later, mangers and horse tackle could still be seen in the building.

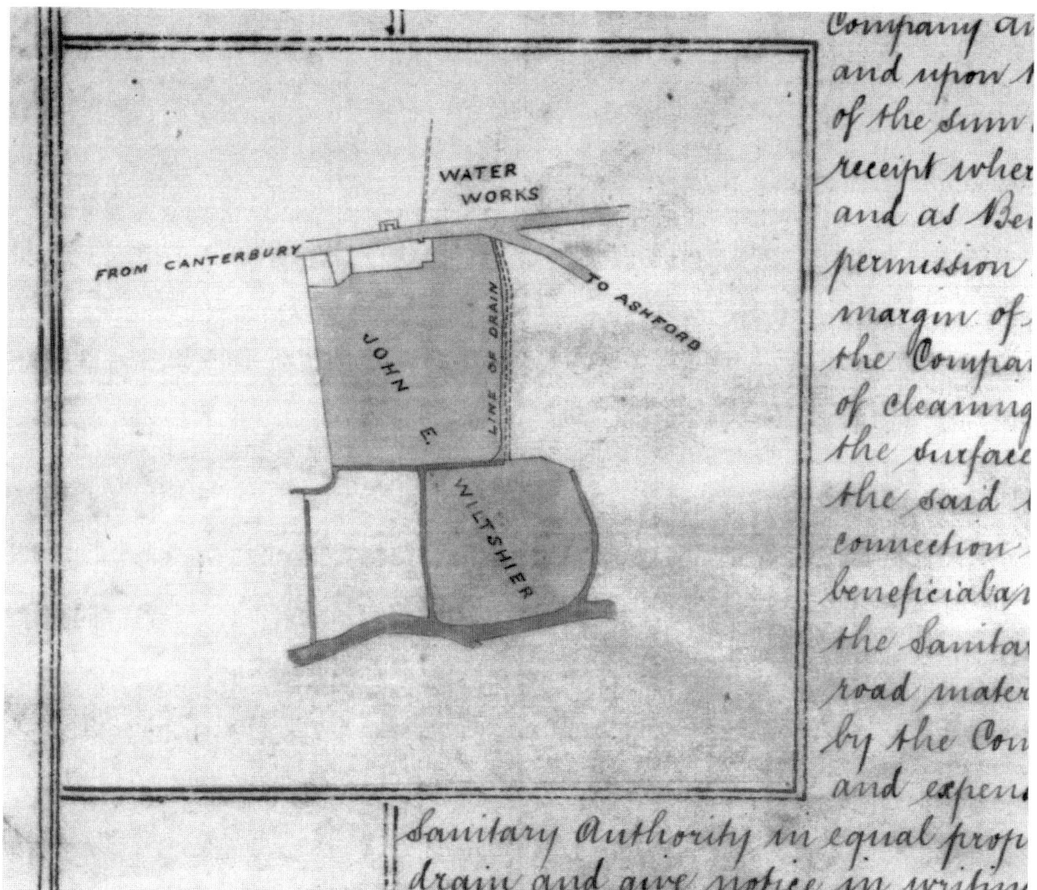

John E. Wiltshier's land at Wincheap in 1888, when the larger of the two fields was rented to George Felix Finn. A map from the property's deeds.

The histories of Robert Brett and George Felix Finn's businesses are closely linked, several of their enginemen and craftsmen moving from one firm to the other. One of them was George Dilnot, who worked for Finn & Co. for 11 years and was one of Robert Brett's drivers for 40 years. After he retired he wrote his reminiscences for Tony Brett, one of Robert's grandsons, and told many stories of Canterbury's steam road locomotive drivers — including Percy Gifford, who always gave his engine 'two or three short sharp bursts, at full throttle, with his head cocked on one side and a cheeky grin on his face' as he drove his Burrell steam tractor up the slope from the railway bridge at the city end of Wincheap.

George recalled that Finn's workshop in Seymour Place had a floor of waterbound flints, a corrugated iron roof, and a few electric lights and power tools. Its electricity came from Canterbury Corporation's generating station in Electric Road, Northgate. Robert's workshops would have been much the same as Finn's. George's reminiscences, and the pictures he gave Tony Brett of Finn's workshops, are priceless insights into the working conditions and practices of those who drove and maintained Canterbury's steam road locomotives.

Elgar Brett (b.1854), Robert's eldest brother, was another of Canterbury's steam road locomotive drivers and by 1889 was married and living with his wife Rosa and children Rose and Elgar (always called 'Dick') in the family's new house at No. 1 Greenfield Terrace, Gordon Road. The house was later renumbered and became No. 17 Gordon Road. Although we do not know who employed him, it is likely that he worked for G.F. Finn. If so, he probably joined Finn several years before Robert and helped him find a job there. In the 1890s Elgar and Rosa had two more children — Agnes and Frank — and moved to a larger house, No. 15 Gordon Road. In about 1912 Elgar started running his own haulage business in Gordon Road. The gap between Nos. 17 and 15 provided access to his depot and also to J.W. Minter & Sons' corn store.

Elgar was nearly 60 years old in 1912 — rather late in life to be setting up a business — but by now Dick was in his mid-20s and Frank was nearly 20, and together they were capable of running the firm under their father's supervision. In addition to taking on haulage work Elgar Brett & Sons were motor engineers. One of their main customers was Frank Cooper (Canterbury) Ltd, who owned a lime quarry in Lime Kiln Road, alongside the Elham Valley Railway, and a building materials yard in Beer Cart Lane.

So, in the years preceding the First World War, we find two brothers — Robert and Elgar — operating as haulage contractors from premises at opposite ends of Wincheap; midway between them is Finn's long-established business, under new ownership. The three companies would have been friendly rivals, but there was enough work to keep all of them busy and occasionally Robert sub-contracted some of his haulage orders to Elgar and Finn's.

Though versatile in many forms of haulage, Finn & Co. is generally remembered as a timber haulier. Robert Brett's fleet also collected and delivered lumber, and had a carpentry department which carried out contract work and built and repaired lorry and trailer bodies, sheds, gates and fences. Phil Sparkes, a sawyer and carpenter at Wincheap Depot from 1926 to 1940, recalled: 'The trunks were collected by Bill

Burchett, one of the strongest men in Canterbury. He drove a Burrell steam tractor and if that couldn't get the trees out, old Bob Brett employed the Gipsons. They had the biggest shire horses I've ever seen. The sawmill was in a shed, about 200 ft long. A 60 hp AC Crompton electric motor drove all the machines. We supplied Dent & Eaton, the wheelwrights in Puckle Lane, and made some big ornamental gates for Bourne Park at Bridge. In about 1932 Mr Bert Brett told me we were packing up all the outside work. I think it was because they wanted the sawmill more for their own use.'

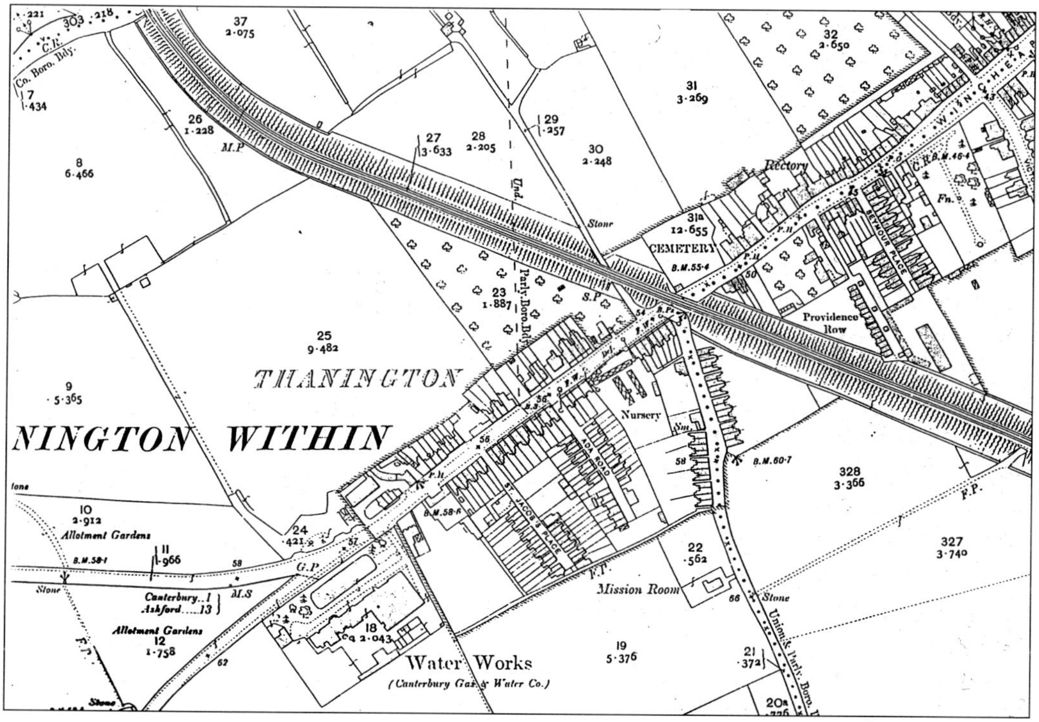

The western end of Wincheap Street, from the Third Edition of the Ordnance Survey (1907). One of the entrances to Finn's workshops — into what later was called 'carpenters' yard' — is immediately adjacent to the '56 ft above sea level' mark. Thanington Cottages are to the right of the workshops, Marlowe Terrace is to the left. The entrance to 'top yard' is to the left of the bench-mark symbol. The field overprinted 'Thanington' is Finn's sports ground. Most of the buildings adjoining its south-east boundary were part of Thanington Engineering Works, later known as Wincheap Depot. *(Canterbury Reference Library)*

OPENING OF THE
NEW ATHLETIC GROUNDS,
WINCHEAP, CANTERBURY,
WHIT-TUESDAY, MAY 15, 1883.

G. F. FINN

Begs to inform the Public that

800 COMPETITORS

Have entered for his benefit,
SUCH AN ENTRY NEVER BEFORE KNOWN.

THE BAND OF THE VOLUNTEERS
From Chatham, under Mr. Williams,

THE BAND OF THE FAVERSHAM VOLUNTEERS,
Under Mr. R. Kempton.

Sports will commence at 11.30. Admission 6d. Grand Stand, 1s. Paddock 1s. One horse Carriages 1s.

COUNTY ATHLETIC GROUNDS,
CANTERBURY.
G. F. FINN, PROPRIETOR.

WHIT-MONDAY,
JUNE 2, 1884.
BICYCLE & TRICYCLE RACES &c.
MILITARY BANDS.
Engagement and First Appearance of

ETHARDO,

The great

SPIRAL ASCENSIONIST,

Who will ascend a Spiral Column 50 feet high, Erected in the centre of the Ground, at 3 & 7 o'clock, And go through his performance, which is a marvel of dexterity, skill and courage.

WHIT-TUESDAY,
JUNE 3.
BICYCLE RACES.
A GREAT
STEEPLECHASE

ETHARDO
AT 2.30 AND 6.30 IN HIS AERIAL ENTERTAINMENT.

WRESTLING BY NOTED WRESTLERS.
Great Military Tournament
BY THE CAVALRY & AUXILIARY FORCES.

G. F. FINN

Has the honour to announce that by the kind permission of the Commanding Officer, Colonel G. R. Fitzroy, the splendid

BAND OF THE COLDSTREAM GUARDS

Will attend and play a selection of choice and popular music on the tennis lawn, under the direction of Mr. C. THOMAS, BANDMASTER.

Accommodation will be provided to seat 1,000 persons to hear this band, free of charge.

Admission 6d. Grand Stand and Paddock 1s. One-horse Carriages 1s.

Canterbury Cycle Club.

COMPETITIONS ON FINN'S GROUND,
THURSDAY, 28TH SEPTEMBER, 1893.

TWO MILES AND A HALF RACE for President's Cup, with a 15s. prize and 10s 6d. prize as usual.

		Gear.	
PHILPOT, E.	Pneumatic.	66	Scratch.
JACKMAN, A. G. P.	"	66	50 yds. start.
WILLIAMS, H.	"	66	90 "
HOLLINGS, H. G.	"	66½	250 "

HALF MILE RACE. Three prizes.

PHILPOT, E.	Scratch.
JACKMAN, A. G. P.	Scratch.
WILLIAMS, H.	Scratch.
HOLLINGS, H. G.	30 yds. start.
GREENWOOD, C. W.	50 "

W. H. OXLEY,
Hon. Sec.

Above left: Announcing the opening of the County Athletic Grounds. From the Kentish Gazette, May 1, 1883. Above: Two days of Whitsun entertainment, advertised in the Kentish Gazette, May 13, 1884. *(Canterbury Reference Library)* **Left: Obviously pneumatic tyres were a novelty when cyclists competed for the President's Cup in 1893.** *(Derek Butler collection)*

The first of a sequence of four photographs from glass negatives discovered in 1995, showing Robert Brett at the controls of one of George Felix Finn's Aveling & Porter traction engines. The engine and its wagons (behind the bushes in the top picture) are collecting 'surface-picked flints' or hand-dug gravel, probably from Covet Wood, Kingston, or nearby Covert Wood. The man with the gun is John White, owner of Reed's Mill, Kingston.

The wagons are now fully-loaded and Robert and his steersman are on their homeward journey, passing Covet Wood Cottage — watched as before by John White.

Another view of the sports meeting and fête first seen on page 11, but here the stage is empty, there are signs of activity at the events notice board on the left (surrounded by hurdles), and trade seems to picking up at the stall in the foreground.

A gymnastics display on the same day.

Another sports day, another gymnastics display. This event took place within a few years of the one featured on the previous page and is seen from the same viewpoint. The pony and cart belong to E. Lukey & Co.

The dense foliage on the trees suggests that this picture was taken at a Whitsun sports day and fête in a year when Whitsun fell in late Spring.

The comparatively empty arena allows us to see an athletics track that ran straight across the centre of the sports field. Steam or smoke rises behind a gap in the trees on the right, perhaps from one of Mr Finn's traction engines, and customers are gathering around the stalls in the foreground.

Here the photographer has focused towards the north-east corner of the arena, giving us a fine view of the Elham Valley Railway embankment and one of Wincheap's gasometers in what is now Jackson Road. The events notice board announces 'Cycling Heat 5' and some of the ladies have raised their parasols on what looks like a typical Edwardian summer's day.

Countdown! Inflating a hot air balloon, a few minutes before a spectacular demonstration. *(collection Canterbury Museums©)* **Top picture: Lift-off! Was this Professor Gyl's or Professor Drake's demonstration? A tiny figure can just be seen dangling beneath the balloon.** *(collection Canterbury Museums©)* **Both pictures are from a collection that belonged originally to Elgar Brett, a keen amateur photographer.**

The Official Programme for the visit of Barnum & Bailey's 'Greatest Show on Earth' to the County Athletic Grounds on July 20, 1899. The acts on the bill included three herds of elephants, human freaks and a team of snake charmers. *(Canterbury Reference Library)*

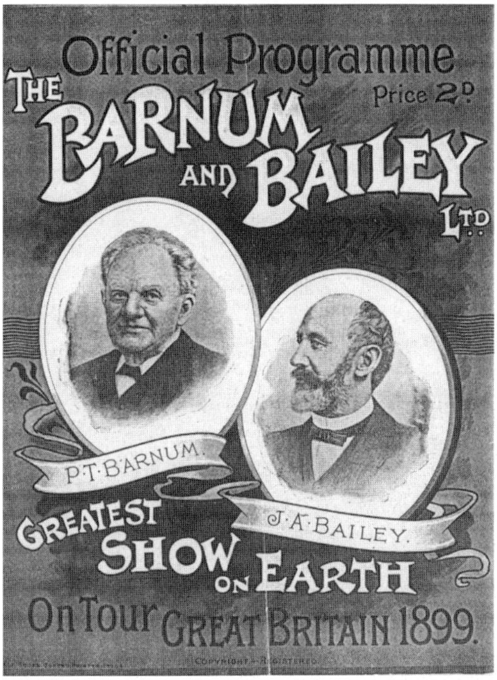

Some of the spectators at this sports day and fête have arrived in what must have been one of the first motor cars to drive to Wincheap. Once again, a gymnastics' display has caught the photographer's attention.

George Felix Finn's Aveling & Porter traction engine no. 2092 and a team of enginemen, photographed a few years before Robert Brett set up his own business. Robert, the engine's driver, is standing fourth from the left. His steersman, Steve Epps, is at the controls. Jack Arman, whose son Arthur ('Jimper') worked for Finn & Co. in Seymour Place, Wincheap, after the First World War, is standing third from the left. The oast house in the background is probably Lillywhite's oast.

Engine no. 2092 and its wagons and water cart outside Canterbury Waterworks, Wincheap. With 'hind wheels' measuring seven feet in diameter, no wonder these vehicles were called 'high wheelers.'

One of G.F. Finn's Thomas Green rollers, probably one of two 8-tonners he bought new in the 1870s, outside one of Wincheap Depot's workshops.

Unidentified enginemen at the depot with what is probably a Burrell traction engine. It carries Finn's nameplate and Canterbury road licence plate No. 21.

Another of G.F. Finn's Thomas Green rollers and an unidentified engineman. The buildings in the background are probably Waterworks Cottages, Wincheap.

One of G.F. Finn's convertible Thomas Green locomotives, fitted with front traction wheels instead of a roller and hauling a Patent Macadam Road Scarifier to break up the road surface before it was remetalled.

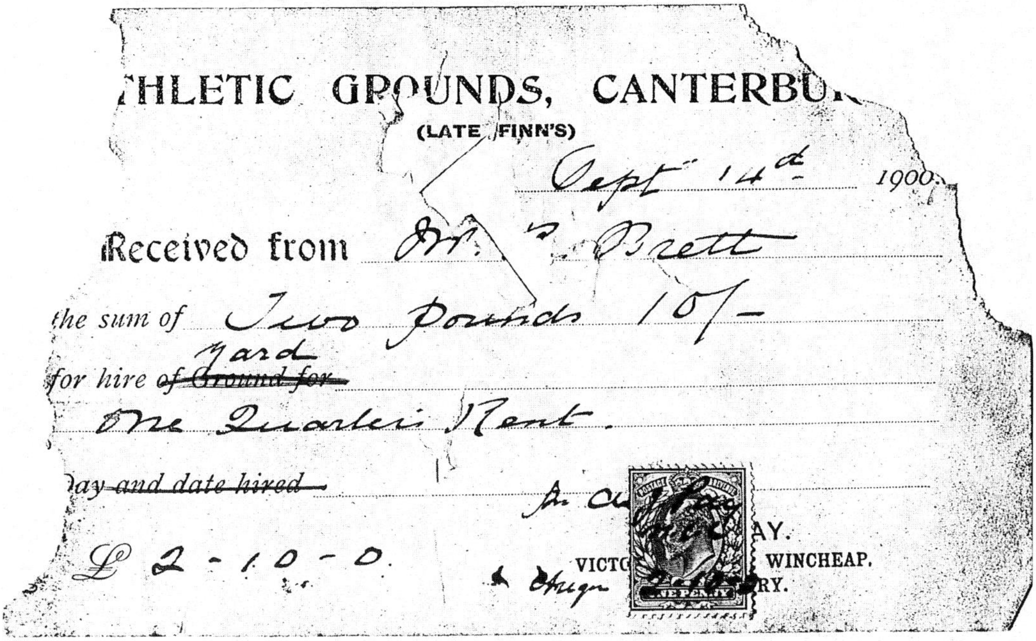

HLETIC GROUNDS, CANTERBU

(LATE FINN'S)

Sept 14th 1900

Received from Mr. Brett

the sum of Two Pounds 10/-

for hire ~~of Ground for~~ Yard

One Quarter's Rent.

Day ~~and date hired~~

£2-10-0

AY.

VICT WINCHEAP.

RY.

The oldest surviving receipt for the rent on what had previously been Finn's yard.

Driver Percy Gifford (left) and his mate and escort 'Jimper' Arman with FN 5011, one of Finn's 10-ton Aveling & Porter steam rollers, built in 1895. This was one of several elderly road engines seen around Canterbury during and after the First World War. By now G.F. Finn had died and his business had been sold and renamed Finn & Co.

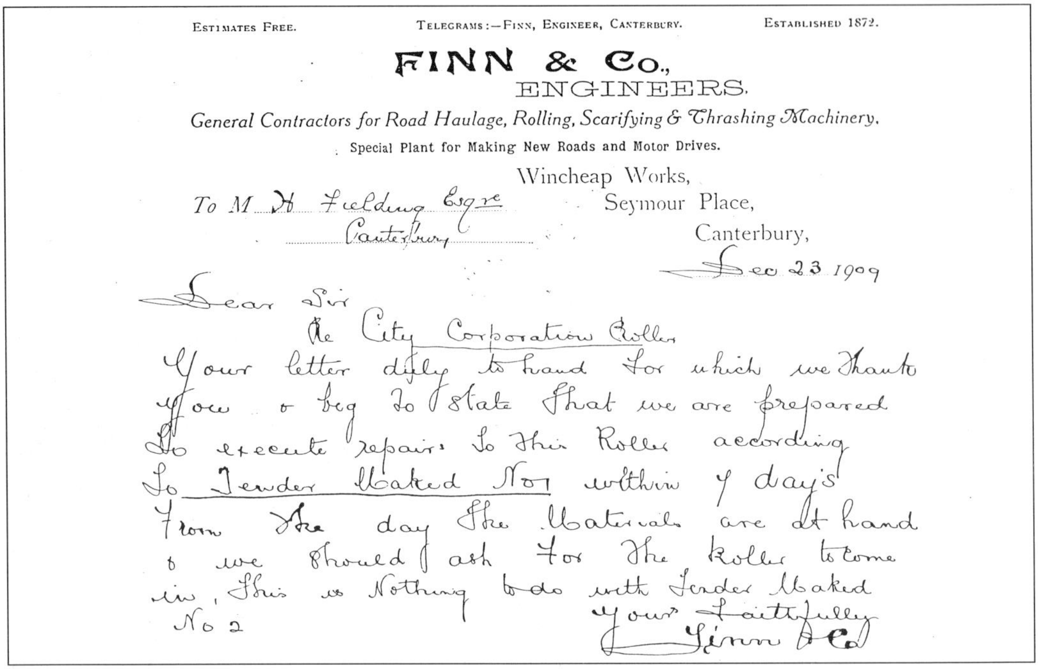

ESTIMATES FREE. TELEGRAMS:—FINN, ENGINEER, CANTERBURY. ESTABLISHED 1872.

FINN & Co.,
ENGINEERS.

General Contractors for Road Haulage, Rolling, Scarifying & Thrashing Machinery.

Special Plant for Making New Roads and Motor Drives.

Wincheap Works,
Seymour Place,
Canterbury,

To M H Fielding Esqre
Canterbury

Dec 23 1909

Dear Sir

Re City Corporation Roller

Your letter duly to hand for which we thank you & beg to state that we are prepared to execute repairs to this Roller according to Tender Marked No 1 within 7 days from the day the materials are at hand & we should ask for the roller to come in, this is nothing to do with Tender Marked No 2

Yours faithfully
Finn & Co

An offer to repair Canterbury Corporation's road roller.

FN 5011 being repaired at Finn's works in Seymour Place, *c.* 1921. Its name plate '289 DERBY COUNTY BOROUGH DERBYSHIRE' identifies a previous owner. In the picture opposite, George Dilnot attends to an electric motor driving a flexible drill with which Steve Epps is drilling-out and tapping firebox stays. In the background, Elgar Brett (right) and possibly his son Frank are standing near the forge. This is a posed photograph; Elgar was probably 'standing in' for an absent Tom Tuppeny, Finn's blacksmith, who lived in Ada Road and also worked for Robert Brett from time to time. The newly shod wheel nearby is probably from a McLaren traction engine owned by Mr Mummery of Bridge. In the picture above, Steve Epps is tapping a stay-hole in the bottom of FN 5011's firebox. The apparatus on the right is an acetylene generator and oxygen cylinder. The gadget above Steve's head consists of a spark plug, a magneto and a handle and allowed him to ignite his oxyacetylene cutter without wasting matches (3d for a dozen boxes!) or burning his fingers.

Top picture: George Dilnot (left) with fellow driver Horace Weatherall at a dinner in 1962, when they received gold watches to commemorate 30 years' service with Bretts.

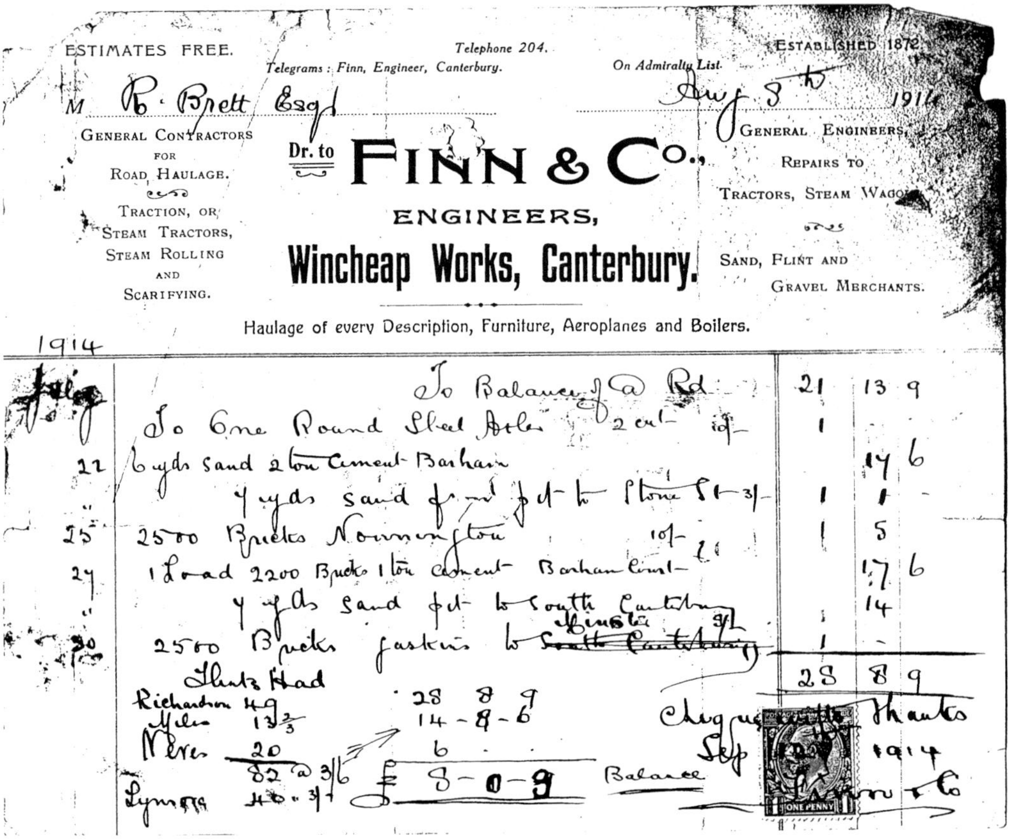

ESTIMATES FREE. Telephone 204. ESTABLISHED 1872.
Telegrams: Finn, Engineer, Canterbury. On Admiralty List.

M R. Brett Esq. Aug 8th 1914

GENERAL CONTRACTORS FOR ROAD HAULAGE. TRACTION, OR STEAM TRACTORS, STEAM ROLLING AND SCARIFYING.

Dr. to FINN & Co., ENGINEERS, Wincheap Works, Canterbury.

GENERAL ENGINEERS, REPAIRS TO TRACTORS, STEAM WAGONS. SAND, FLINT AND GRAVEL MERCHANTS.

Haulage of every Description, Furniture, Aeroplanes and Boilers.

1914		£	s. d.
July	To Balance of a/c Rd	21	13 9
	To One Round Steel Axle 2 cwt	1	- -
22	6 yds sand 2 ton Cement Barham		14 6
"	4 yds sand fm pit to Stone St 3/-	1	1 -
25	2500 Bricks Nonnington 10/-	1	5
27	1 Load 2200 Bricks 1 ton Cement Barham Court		17 6
"	4 yds sand pit to South Canterbury		14
30	2500 Bricks [illegible] to ~~South Canterbury~~	1	-
		28	8 9

Thats Had
Richardson 49 ... 28 8 9
Miles 13 2/3 ... 14 - 8 - 6
Neves 20 ... 6
82 @ 3/6 ... £ 8 - 0 - 9 Balance
Lynsted 40 @ 3/-

Cheque with thanks Sep 1914 Finn & Co

An invoice from Finn & Co. to Robert Brett, for delivering building materials to Barham, Nonington and South Canterbury.

'Where am I going?' yelled driver George Frederick Dilnot (George Dilnot's father) as Finn's Burrell traction engine Little Belgian slipped into the River Medway on July 20, 1928, while he was delivering tree trunks to the London & Rochester Trading Company. The engine was recovered next day and driven back to Wincheap, the only evidence of the accident being a bent front axle. Opposite page: Finn's Burrell Gold Medal steam tractor Charlie at The Sign of the Gate, Old Dover Road, Canterbury, *c.* 1920. Charlie was being driven from The Wilderness, Nackington, to Tolputt's sawmills in Maison Dieu Road, Dover, by George Frederick Dilnot; his mate, Tom White, is sitting on the tree trunk. Below: an invoice from Robert Brett to Elgar Brett for delivering beer to Folkestone.

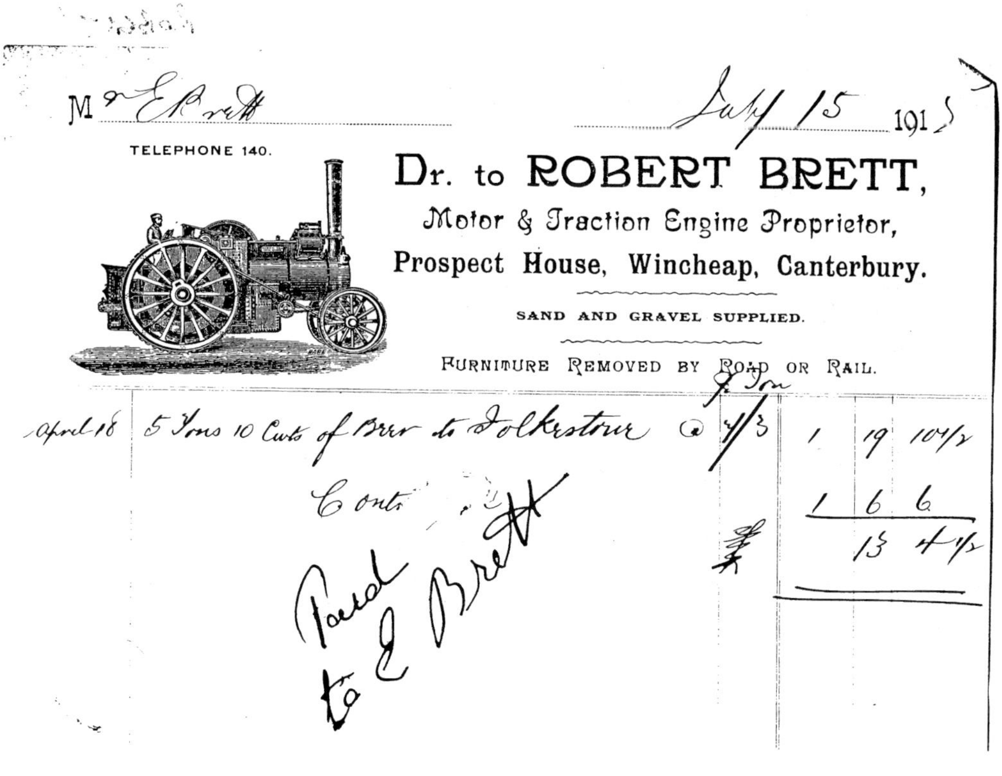

M^r E Brett   July 15 1915

TELEPHONE 140.

Dr. to ROBERT BRETT,

Motor & Traction Engine Proprietor,

Prospect House, Wincheap, Canterbury.

SAND AND GRAVEL SUPPLIED.

FURNITURE REMOVED BY ROAD OR RAIL.

April 18	5 Tons 10 Cwts of Beer to Folkestone @ 7/3	1	19	10½
	Contra	1	6	6
			13	4½

Paid to E Brett

Elgar Brett's Tasker traction engine AA 5013 (works no. 1488), bought new in February 1912, setting off on a delivery round for one of Canterbury's breweries. Elgar's son Dick is third from the left. One of the enginemen's destinations may have been the Hop Poles pub in Wincheap, which sold Ash ales and stout. *(Jean Lynes collection)*

Mr R. Brett.

Dr. to ELGAR BRETT,

MOTOR • HAULAGE • CONTRACTOR,

15, GORDON ROAD, CANTERBURY.

1912		£	s	d
Mar 19.	Building Mat Brownings to Knowlton sleepers Higham to Mounts	1	18	0
" 23	Pipes Whitstable to Mount. 6 Tons	1	1	0
25	Iron Whitstable to Begglestons 6 Tons	1	1	0
" 26 to 30	6 Ton Tiles Reading to Sandwich / Scaffolding Sandwich to Barham	13	19	-
Apr 6	Pipes Whitstable to Howfield	1	2	0
" 20	Roots Hackington to Calcott 6 Tons	1	4	0
May 1	8 yds Sand St Stephens to Barham	1	-	-
		£21	5	-

Cheques ... with Thanks

HALFPENNY HALFPENNY

An advertisement for Bretts' timber services, published in the 1920s or early 1930s. Opposite page: An invoice from Elgar Brett to Robert for delivering building materials.

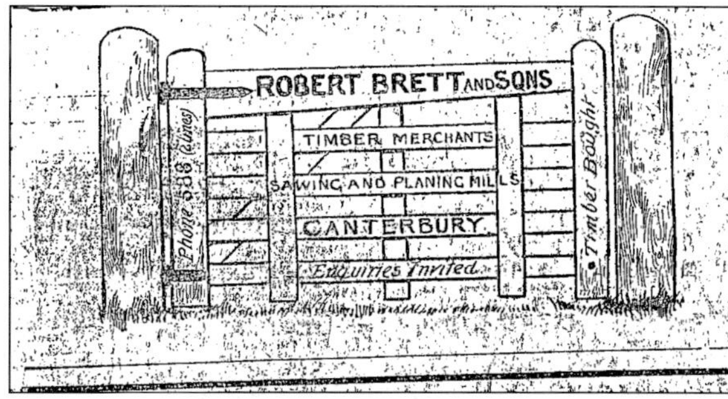

Timber hauliers, perhaps working for Gipson Brothers of Shalmsford Street, Chartham, in Wincheap in 1923. The team has just passed the entrance to Wincheap Depot's 'top yard' and is probably heading for Finn & Co's yard in Seymour Place, which sawed bulk timber, or W.J. Payne's timber yard in King Street, on the other side of Canterbury. Waterworks Cottages are on the far left, next door to No. 108 Wincheap, occupied by Frank Makey at the time this picture was taken. The Hop Poles (licensee: L. Dove) was well situated for passing and local trade. It was the 'first and last' pub for travellers approaching and leaving Canterbury via Wincheap. There would have been a daily gathering of thirsty workers from Wincheap Depot, the oast house, Canterbury Waterworks, Thanington Dairy and nearby farms; and at evenings and weekends the bar would have been crowded with 'locals' playing darts or dominoes. The tenants of the three cottages to the right of the pub were Charles Phipps (No. 106 Wincheap), E.G. Whittaker (No. 105) and William Iddenden (No. 104). The cottages were previously known as Nos. 7, 6 and 5 Marlowe Terrace.

Another fascinating picture from Canterbury's steam road locomotive era. The picture belonged originally to Elgar Brett and was probably taken by him. Although the load, location and enginemen have not been identified it is likely that the Aveling & Porter engine was part of his fleet. It is possible that the photograph was taken during a haulage job for his brother Robert. *(Jean Lynes collection)*

Our final picture in this section was also originally in Elgar Brett's collection and was taken when the 'green shoots' of Finn's athletics enterprise and haulage business at Wincheap were well established. The trees, among them the poplars that Robert Brett help to plant in 1884, now dominate the sky-line. The first of the white picket fences that became a feature of the west side of the ground has been erected. *(collection Canterbury Museums ©)*

2: Grass roots

Wincheap Depot and the surrounding area more than 60 years ago. 'Top yard' provides a convenient reference point for comparing this rather tattered picture with the aerial view on page 2. A steam roller heads towards Thanington, passing the Partington Kent Bill Posting Company's hoarding between the gates that led into 'top yard.' Hop gardens and Canterbury Waterworks dominate the foreground. On the right, behind Lillywhite's oast house, Bretts' timber yard occupies the edge of the disused sports ground. Photographed by Surrey Air Services operating from The London Terminal Aerodrome, Croydon. *(David Swain collection)*

WHILE establishing his haulage business, Robert Brett bought seven Burrell traction engines in a period of five years. The first was a large 'contractor's-type' machine of ten nominal horse power, built in 1898 and acquired second-hand in March 1909. His next vehicle, no. 1480 in Burrell's works records, was even older. It was built in 1890 for Gardner & Co., brewers, of Ash-next-Sandwich, and purchased from the Wingham Engineering Co. in April 1910.

At about this time, according to one of the stories that Canterbury's steam enginemen used to tell, Robert invited a driver known as 'Dover Bill' Setterfield, previously employed by Baldocks of Dover, to become his business partner. Setterfield declined, but evidently worked for Robert for a time as driver of '1480.' He is at the controls in our picture on the opposite page, taken when the engine paraded through Canterbury decorated with 'Jack's Winning' banners during the December 1910 General Election campaign. Robert supported John ('Jack') Hennicker Heaton (Conservative), who lost by 472 votes to Francis Bennett-Goldney (Independent Unionist).

When Robert worked for G.F. Finn, one of his jobs was to collect 'surface picked flints' from farms on the North Downs. The flints were turned up in abundance when the fields were ploughed, and sold for 6s 6d a cubic yard to local councils, for building and repairing roads. When Robert set up his own business he too went into the flint trade.

To finance his business until it became profitable, Robert had to borrow money, and everyone in his family who was old enough to work had to contribute to the household's income. Reminiscing in later life, Bert Brett recalled: 'We had a big green vegetable round ... and kept pigs. We [children] all had to do something ... either weeding or keeping the bees from swarming or taking the pigs to market.'

Robert Brett jnr (b. 1890), the eldest of Robert and Emma's four sons, was the first to join the family firm, working as a traction engine driver until leaving to run grocery shops in Canterbury and Thanet. He returned later as the company's representative in the Thanet area, retiring in 1956. He moved to Canada in 1967 and died there in 1975. Robert and Emma's other sons — William (b. 1893), Thomas (b. 1896) and Bert (b. 1900) — also joined the firm. Thomas served in the Royal Flying Corps during the First World War and died in 1919 from mastoiditis. Recalling, over 40 years later, how he and Tom fitted new shoes to traction engine wheels in the blacksmith's shop, Bert said: 'My job in those days was rivet boy. I used to carry the hot rivets from the forge to the wheel. I can always remember my brother Tom stripped to the waist, perspiration pouring off him ... we hardly stopped for food. In those days we used to try and set records to see just how quickly we could shoe the big wheels.'

When Robert jnr, William, Thomas and Bert started to take on their share of the firm's work, Robert named his business 'Robert Brett & Sons.' In 1911 he opened a head office at No. 1 St Margaret's Street, Canterbury, but continued to handle some of his paperwork from an office in a shed at Wincheap Depot.

The shed was the domain of Thomas Boys Gambrill, Bretts' chief engineer and works manager, who joined the firm in 1912. He was probably Robert's first recruit from outside the family and certainly his first long-service employee. Tom Gambrill came from a family which had steam in its blood. His father, Thomas Henry ('Old Harry') Gambrill, ran a steam haulage, sawing, ploughing and threshing business from Mill House, near the Chequers pub on the Stone Street at Petham. When they left school both Tom and his brother, 'Young Harry', joined their father's business. 'Old Harry' was a demanding employer and one day he and Tom had an argument, after which Tom went to Wincheap and persuaded Robert to give him a job at the very time when the grass roots of Robert's business were becoming established. Tom and another of Robert's engineers, George Young, set up Brett's first mechanised quarry, in Swanton Lane, Littlebourne. Skips hauled by locomotives carried the gravel from the quarry face to a crushing and grading plant, which was driven by an old Fowler traction engine.

In the early 1920s Tom Gambrill and his wife Emily lived at No. 4 Thanington Cottages, the Brett family's old address, later moving to Ulmarra, a bungalow near St Nicholas' Church, Thanington. Emily died in 1938; Tom retired in 1939 due to ill-health, following an accident at home, and died in 1948 at the age of 66. The Gambrills' graves, and those of several members of the Brett family and employees of the firm, can be found in the church's burial ground.

Left to right: Robert Brett, founder of Robert Brett & Sons; Robert Brett jnr; Tom Brett.

One of Robert's Burrell traction engines in St Dunstan's Street, Canterbury, in 1910, hauling woolsacks for G.W. Green & Sons, wool merchants, of Kirby's Lane and North Lane, Canterbury. *(Saunders, Canterbury)*

This John Fowler Class A7 steam engine (works number 13149), built in 1913, was owned by Robert Brett from *c.* 1916 until 1918 and was one of three Fowlers he bought during or immediately after the Great War. No. 13149 previously belonged to W. Vousden of Eastry. 'Old Harry' Gambrill (seated) and Dick Francis are at the controls. Their presence in the picture is something of a mystery, since so far as is known 13149 was never part of the Gambrill fleet. *(Hilary Wood collection)*

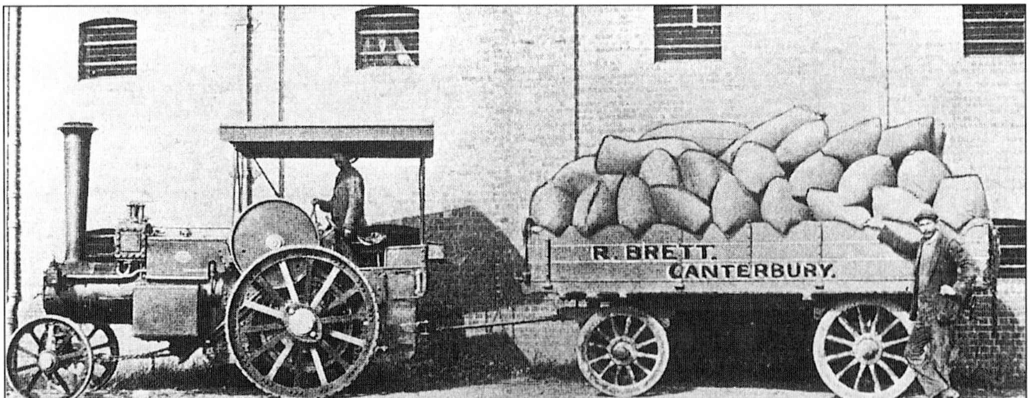

Another of Robert's Burrell engines, hauling hop pockets or sacks of wool or chaff. This picture was first published in Burrell's Gold Medal tractor catalogue.

G.F. Finn and Robert Brett's former workshops in 1987. The corrugated iron building in the foreground was the traction engine repair shop and forge, and later became the carpenters' shop. Beyond it are 'carpenters' yard' and its entrance from Wincheap. No. 4 Thanington Cottages is to the left of the yard, No. 1 Marlowe Terrace to the right.

This five-ton chain-driven Burrell steam wagon, bought on January 21, 1913, was the thirteenth to be built to a design based on Burrell's highly successful Gold Medal steam tractor. The wagon was one of two Burrells that Robert bought new, the other being a 1915 five-ton steam tractor. Burrell wagons never became as popular as Fodens, which Robert bought in ever-increasing numbers after the First World War.

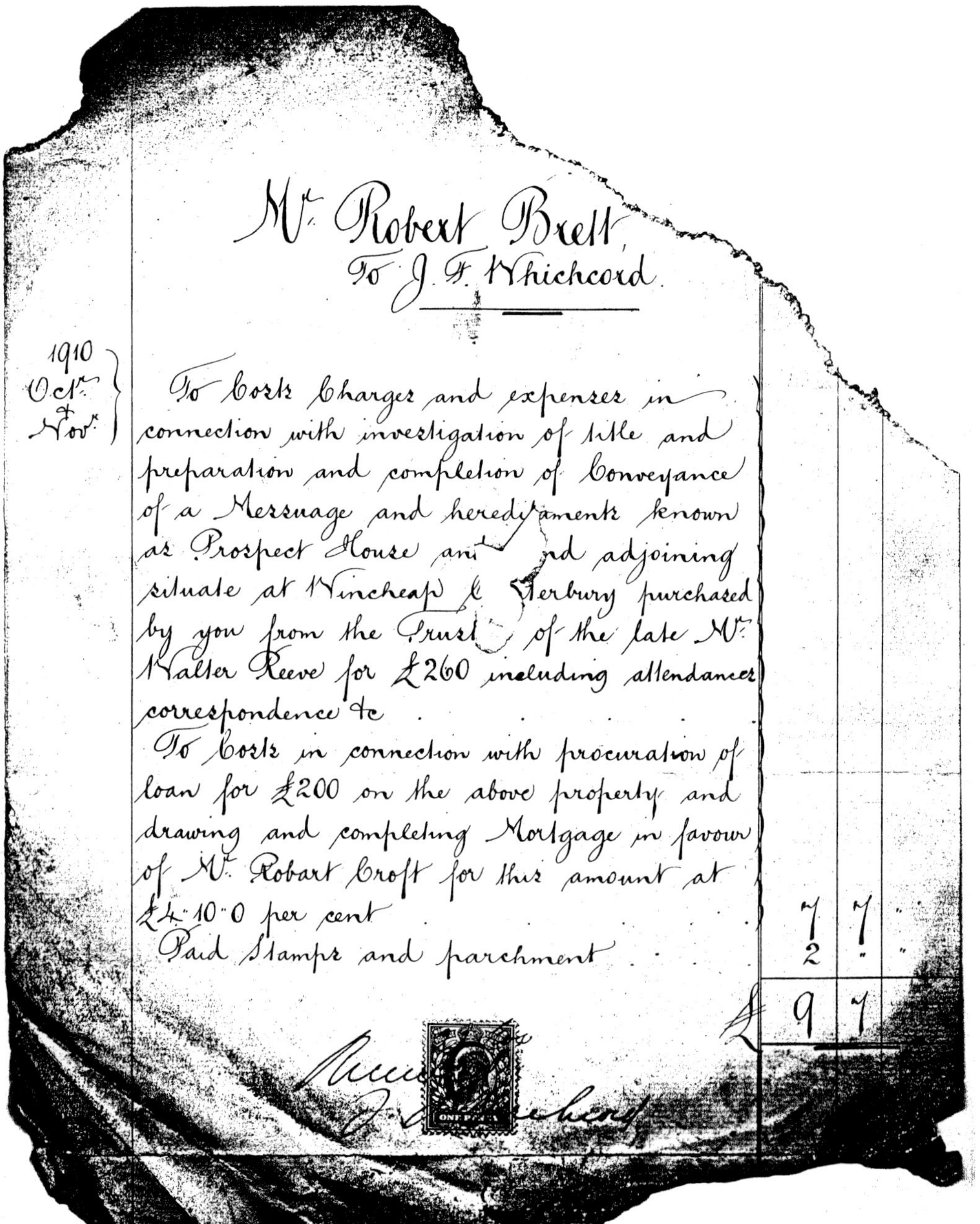

Mr. Robert Brett,
To J. F. Whichcord.

1910 Octr. & Novr. — To Costs Charges and expenses in connection with investigation of title and preparation and completion of Conveyance of a Messuage and hereditaments known as Prospect House an[illegible]nd adjoining situate at Wincheap C[illegible]terbury purchased by you from the Trust[illegible] of the late Mr. Walter Reeve for £260 including attendances correspondence &c . . . . .

To Costs in connection with procuration of loan for £200 on the above property and drawing and completing Mortgage in favour of Mr. Robert Croft for this amount at £4"10"0 per cent . . . . . 7 7 "

Paid Stamps and parchment . . . . . 2 " "

£ 9 7

Rece[illegible]
J. [illegible]chcord

After renting Prospect House for two years Robert bought the property for £260.

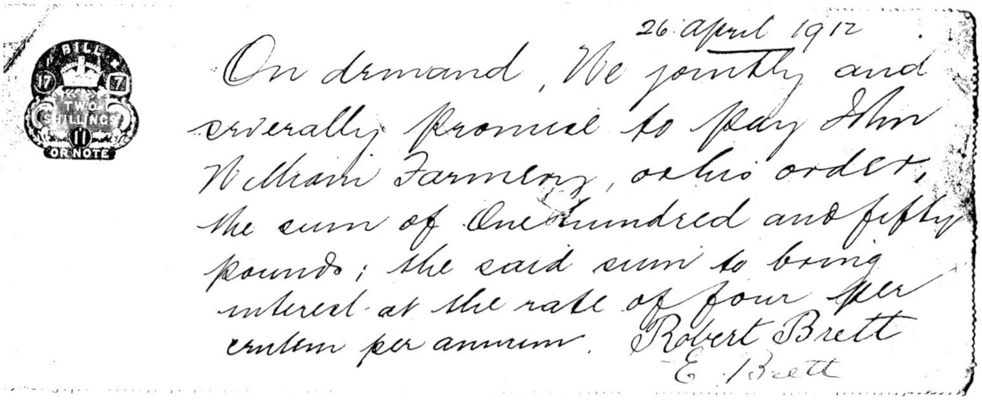

In April 1912 retired Chief Constable J.W. Farmery lent Robert and Emma £150 at 4 per cent p.a. They repaid the loan in August 1914.

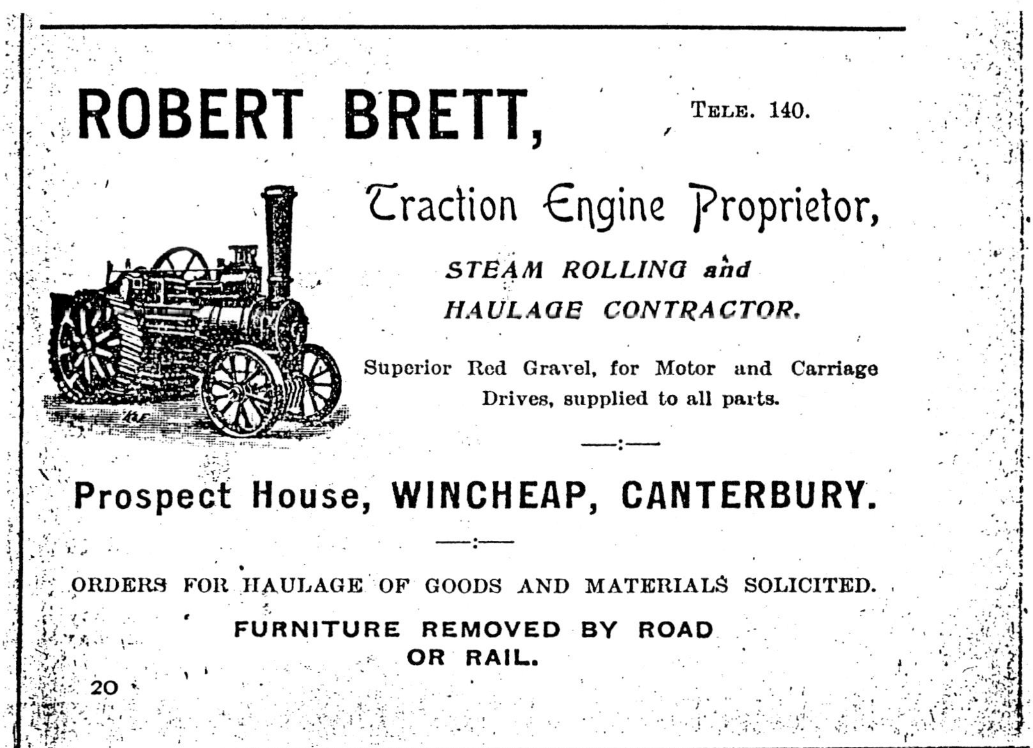

Robert's first advertisement, from 'Pike's Blue Book', 1910.

Tom Gambrill (left) and carpenter Phil Sparkes at Ulmarra. Thanington in the 1930s.

One of Robert Brett's timber wagons at Wincheap Depot, with driver Harry Hadlow. *(Richard Woods collection)*

Family snaps taken in Wincheap back gardens in the 1920s and 1930s. Bert Brett (left) and his brother William are seen at Prospect House, on the garden path that led to a gate into 'bottom yard.' The Elham Valley Railway embankment is beyond the trees. The second picture, taken in about 1937, shows Bert and Winifred Brett's daughter Barbara (left) with Barbara Weatherall and Gerald Ackroyd, whose fathers worked at Bretts. No. 4 Thanington Cottages is on the right (partly obscured by the forge seen on page 39), Prospect House is at the opposite end of the row. *(Barbara Tilly collection)*

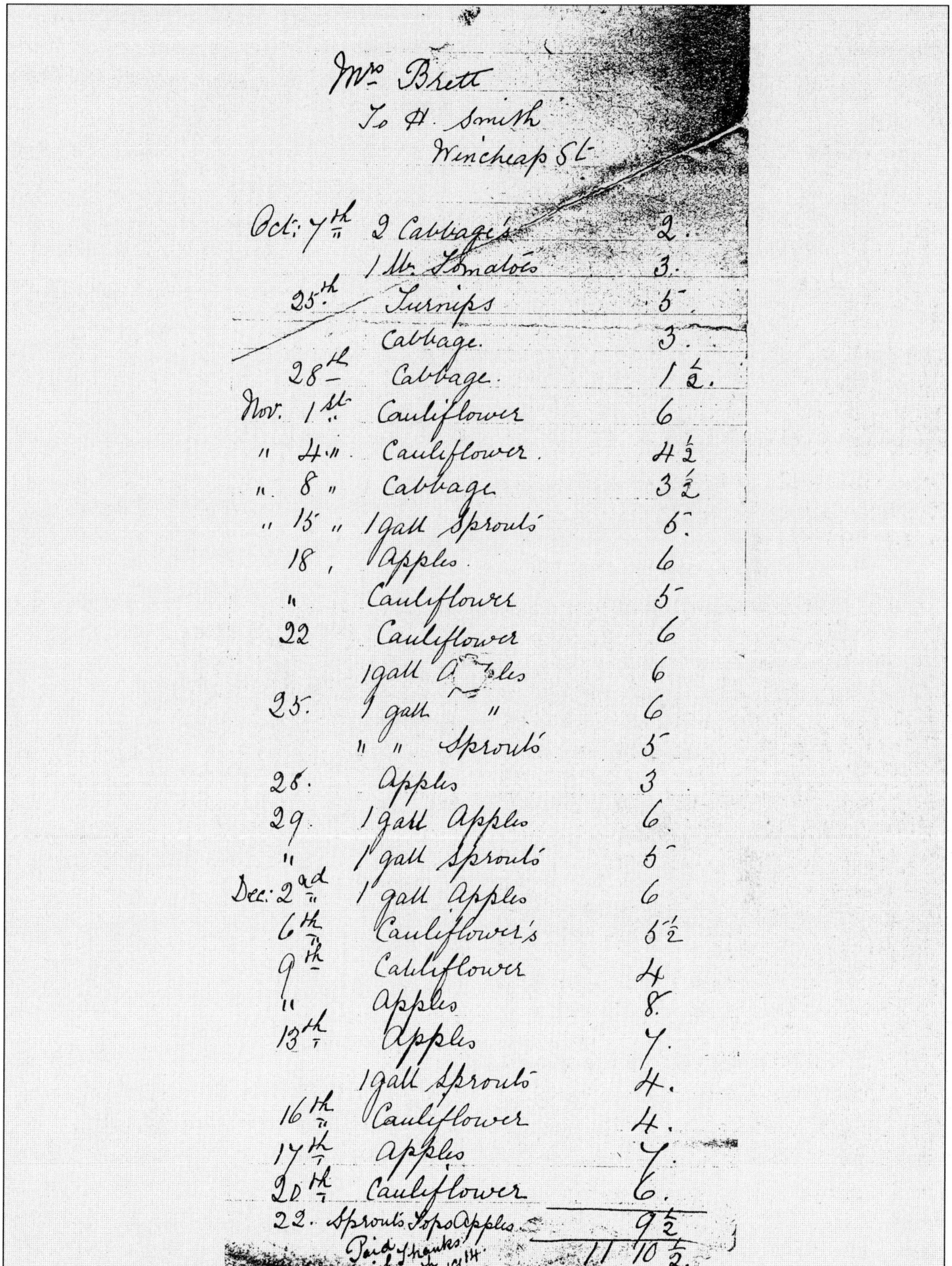

Mrs Brett
To H. Smith
Wincheap St

Oct: 7th	2 Cabbage's	2.
	1 lb Tomatoes	3.
25th	Turnips	5.
	Cabbage.	3.
28th	Cabbage.	1½.
Nov. 1st	Cauliflower	6
" 4 "	Cauliflower.	4½
" 8 "	Cabbage	3½
" 15 "	1 gall Sprouts	5.
18 ,	Apples.	6
"	Cauliflower	5
22	Cauliflower	6
	1 gall Apples	6
25.	1 gall "	6
	" " Sprouts	5
26.	Apples	3
29.	1 gall Apples	6.
"	1 gall Sprouts	5
Dec: 2nd	1 gall Apples	6
6th	Cauliflower's	5½
9th	Cauliflower	4
"	Apples	8.
13th	Apples	7.
	1 gall Sprouts	4.
16th	Cauliflower	4.
17th	Apples	7.
20th	Cauliflower	6.
22.	Sprouts Tops Apples	9½
		11 10½

Paid with thanks
[illegible] 17th 1914

A bill for three months' greengroceries for 11s 10½d. Emma Brett sold produce from the garden and orchard behind Prospect House to help the family make ends meet. 'H. Smith' was probably Henry Smith of Hope Cottage, 87 Wincheap Street.

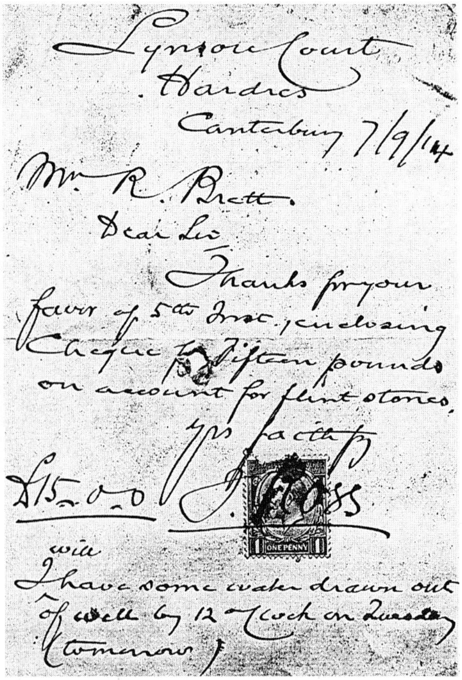

Lynsore Court
Hardres
Canterbury 7/9/14

Mr R. Brett.

Dear Sir

Thanks for your favor of 5th Inst. enclosing Cheque for Fifteen pounds on account for flint stones.

Yrs faithfy
[illegible]

£15-0-0

ONE PENNY

will have some water drawn out of well by 12 o'clock on Tuesday (tomorrow)

Lynsore Court, on the North Downs, was one of Robert's sources of flints and had a well from which he drew water for his engines.

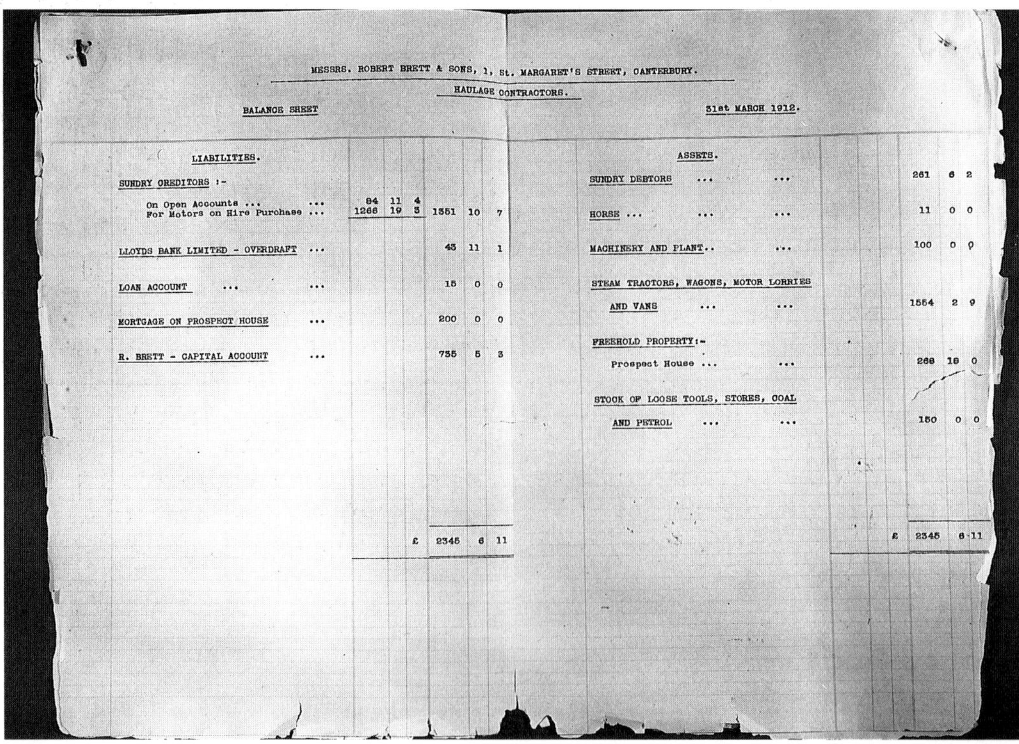

MESSRS. ROBERT BRETT & SONS, 1, St. MARGARET'S STREET, CANTERBURY.

HAULAGE CONTRACTORS.

BALANCE SHEET — 31st MARCH 1912.

LIABILITIES.							ASSETS.			
SUNDRY CREDITORS :-							SUNDRY DEBTORS	261	6	2
On Open Accounts	84	11	4							
For Motors on Hire Purchase ...	1266	19	3	1351	10	7	HORSE	11	0	0
LLOYDS BANK LIMITED - OVERDRAFT ...				43	11	1	MACHINERY AND PLANT.. ...	100	0	0
LOAN ACCOUNT				15	0	0	STEAM TRACTORS, WAGONS, MOTOR LORRIES AND VANS	1554	2	9
MORTGAGE ON PROSPECT HOUSE ...				200	0	0	FREEHOLD PROPERTY:-			
R. BRETT - CAPITAL ACCOUNT ...				735	5	3	Prospect House	268	18	0
							STOCK OF LOOSE TOOLS, STORES, COAL AND PETROL	150	0	0
			£	2345	6	11	£	2345	6	11

Robert Brett & Sons' first balance sheet. Assets include more than £1500-worth of steam and motor vehicles, and £11-worth of real horse power!

3: Steaming along Wincheap

A classic photograph from Canterbury's industrial past, taken at Wincheap Depot on a Saturday morning *c.* 1930 after Bretts' drivers had completed their weekly washing duties. The vehicles in the foreground are five-ton Foden steam wagons. The two on the right were built in the First World War and were among several ex-War Department and Admiralty vehicles that Bretts bought in the 1920s. The third wagon from the right is of similar vintage, while the next one along is a 1927 model bought in February 1928. The next four are 1928 or 1929 models, purchased new. The vehicles in the back row are mostly motor lorries, some or all of which were 'ex-WD.' A traction engine or steam roller (under a tarpaulin) and two more steam lorries, one carrying a tank, are on the far left. *(B.& W. Fisk-Moore)*

FOR 50 years Wincheap was imbued with the sight, sound and sooty aroma of steam locomotives and wagons as they set out from 'top yard' in the early morning, returned 12 or more hours later, and parked in neat rows while being prepared for the next day's work. Initially the fleet consisted mainly of Burrells but between 1917 and 1929 about 20 Foden wagons were acquired, as well as a number of motor lorries, including war-surplus American Peerless, Garford and Liberty trucks.

Everyone who remembers Wincheap Depot in those days recalls Jack Arter, the 'yard man', who lived at No. 19 Claremont Place and always came to work with string tied round his trousers, below the knees — as if to prevent rats running up his legs! Jack started work between 3 and 4 o'clock in the morning, his first job being to light the fires in the Fodens and make sure that they were steamed up and ready to go when the enginemen reported for work at 6. When motor lorries superseded the steam wagons Jack still had to make an early start: in winter, the lorries' radiators were emptied every night and Jack had to fill them with hot water next morning.

When 'clocking in' was introduced, Jack was issued with clock-card number one. After he retired it was allocated to Jack Martin, who joined Central Workshops as a motor fitter in 1947.

The engine drivers were instructed to drive carefully and courteously, and were obliged to keep their vehicles in impeccable condition. The depot's instruction book contained 75 rules, one of which stated: 'If any driver is not satisfied with his mate he must inform us the reason.' Bert Brett, who was in charge of production, engineering and transport, inspected every lorry after the Saturday morning 'wash-down' and never failed to spot the tiniest defect; not even the smallest stone embedded in a tyre escaped his eye.

On January 11, 1928, Robert Brett & Sons became a limited company and acquired substantial assets previously owned by Robert Brett. These included the freehold of the Wincheap site (which Robert had bought in 1919); gravel pits at Oldridge Wood, Littlebourne ('Swanton Pit'), Kingston ('Kingston Pit'), Riverdale Road, Canterbury ('Inge's Pit'), and Barton Mills, Canterbury ('Barton Pit'); and gravel-bearing land on the outskirts of Canterbury at Howfield Wood, Chartham, and Hoad's Wood, Sturry.

The firm described itself as a 'Haulage and General Contractor, Quarry Owner, Gravel and Stone Merchant and Timber Merchant.' Robert snr, William and Bert Brett were the main shareholders. Tom Gambrill received a small block of shares, in recognition of his contribution to the firm's success. Wincheap Depot continued to expand, servicing transport and machinery for the firm's many businesses.

In 1928 the firm won a contract from South Eastern Tar Distillers Ltd ('SETAR') to carry crude tar from gas works in Kent to SETAR's refinery in Broad Oak Road, Canterbury, and deliver tanks and drums of refined tar to the gangs who tarred and gritted the roads for Kent County Council and the county's local councils. A fleet of Foden steam wagons equipped to carry tar took its place alongside the sand and gravel and general haulage lorries at Wincheap Depot. Though owned by Bretts, the tar wagons bore SETAR's livery — an early example of a haulage contractor 'dedicating' part of its fleet of vehicles to one customer. The first Foden tar tankers (FN 9175 and FN 9176) were delivered in April 1928, followed by another tank wagon and three tipper wagons in July. In May 1929 Bretts bought a Foden wagon (JG 90) with interchangeable bodies (one for carrying a tank, the other for barrels) to deliver tar in the Tonbridge area.

Above: Jack Arter and his son Sydney, one of Bretts' enginemen, in their Sunday best with FN 9176, a brand new Foden wagon, at Wincheap Depot, Whitsun 1928. This must have been one of the last Fodens to have solid tyres. FN 9176's regular driver was Tom Dicker. An ex-War Department Foden bought in 1927 stands alongside. Several one hundredweight bags of coal are stacked beside the fence. Each Foden set off for its day's work with nine bags. *(Christine Pope collection)*
Right: HO 5528, purchased in 1925, and five other Fodens at the depot. *(Christine Pope collection)*

On the road *c.* 1930 with Foden wagons AA 2001 and M 6872. The enginemen have pulled in to brew some tea and draw water from a ditch. M 6872 was an ex-Admiralty wagon, built in 1914 and bought by Bretts in 1925. *(Christine Pope collection)*

Driver George Knight (left) and Fred ('Cut') Rye (right) with an unidentified engineman. The only clues that may help identify the location are the milestone or boundary stone in front of the vehicle, and the metal signs behind the trailer. The diamond-shaped sign was a weight restriction notice and was once a common sight on bridges over the Elham Valley Railway and other railways around Canterbury. One wonders whether this 'wagon train' complied with the restriction! *(Christine Pope collection)*

Bretts' second Foden steam wagon, built in 1913 and bought from D. Cottingham & Sons of Horsham in 1918. The man on the left is probably driver Alf Harris, who lived in Faversham.

Unidentified enginemen or farm workers with a load of woolsacks on an ex-WD Foden wagon built in 1917. Bretts bought the wagon in about 1922, possibly at a sale of ex-Army vehicles at Richborough Port, near Sandwich.

A Foden wagon, bought new in April 1928, drawing water while working for SETAR. Few journeys could be made without refilling the engine's water tank along the way. A stream at Sarre was a popular topping-up stop between Canterbury and the Thanet towns.

Driver Percy Blunt with his Foden tar wagon and Blean District Council roadmen near the Knaves Ash pub, Hoath, in 1930. The vehicle is a 1918 ex-War Department wagon, bought in 1927. The picture was taken soon after Percy had delivered a load of tar for repairing the road.

Foden JG 90, equipped with its articulated body for carrying drums of tar.

Drums of refined tar at SETAR's refinery in Broad Oak Road, Canterbury, ready to be collected by Wincheap Depot's Foden wagons one day in the late 1920s or early 1930s. The man on the motor cycle is refinery manager Ron Gant.

Bretts' Aveling & Porter steam roller (works number 11055, registration no. NY 6931) at Nethercourt Circus, Ramsgate, in 1935, when George Dilnot was its regular driver. The roller was built in 1924. Robert Brett bought it from W.H. Wilkinson of Llantwit Major, Glamorgan, in October 1928 for contract work on waterbound-macadam and tar-macadam roads. (*Audrey Gilham collection*)

Fred Rye (right) and W. Wilsden with a 1914 Foden, bought from the Western Motor Wagon Company in 1922.

Foden FN 8752, driven by Charlie Stace, marooned in floodwater in Fordwich Road, Sturry, while on its way back to Wincheap Depot during the winter of 1927/8. Photographed by Wallace Mumford.

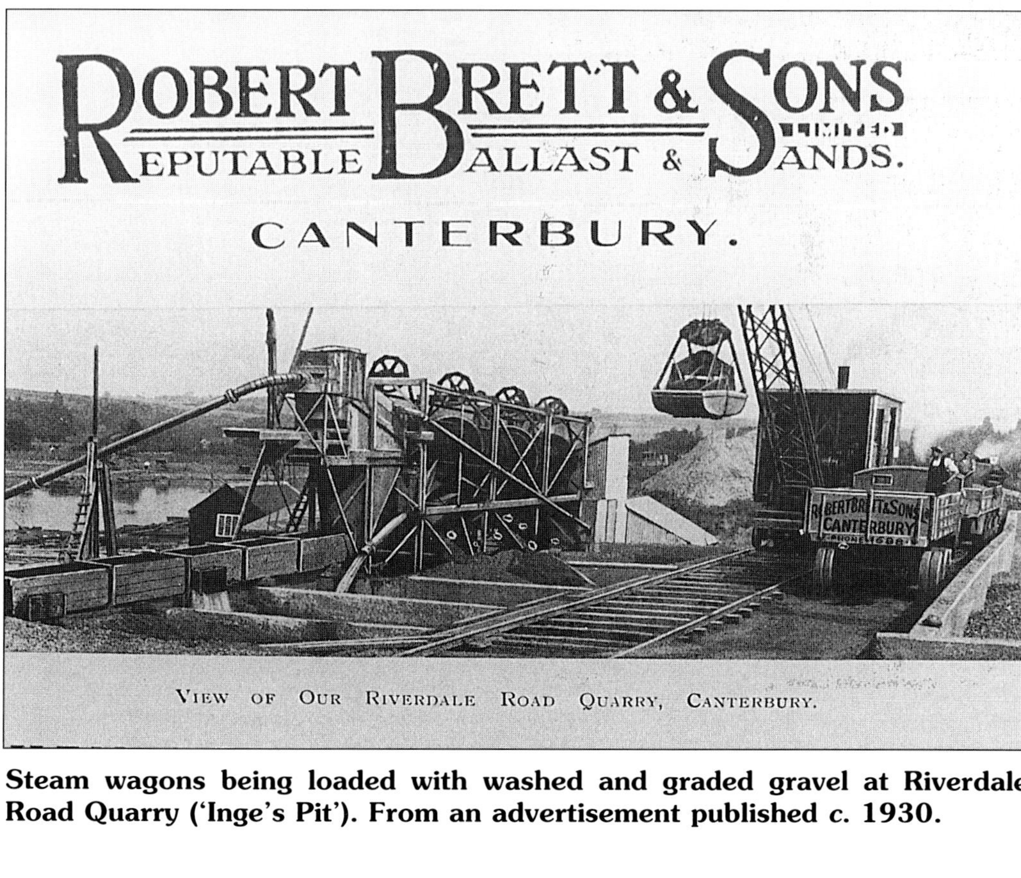

Steam wagons being loaded with washed and graded gravel at Riverdale Road Quarry ('Inge's Pit'). From an advertisement published *c.* 1930.

ROBERT BRETT & SONS

LIMITED.

SAND and BALLAST
: QUARRY OWNERS :

BUILDING & ROAD MAKING MATERIALS
always in stock.

ROAD TRANSPORT
: CONTRACTORS :

Petrol & Steam Vehicles for Hire from 10 cwts. to 10 tons

REMOVAL CONTRACTORS

Special Furniture Vans for
Long Distance Removals.

Specialists in Ferro-Concrete Materials

Works & Depot: Wincheap Street,

Offices: 1 St. Margaret's Street,

CANTERBURY.

Telegrams : "Haulage." Telephone : 588

From the programme for the Canterbury Operatic Society's 1928 production of HMS Pinafore. The advertisement lists the many services offered by Bretts — all of which were keeping Wincheap Depot busier than ever.

4: The first motor lorries

Hauling woolsacks, *c.* 1930. By now, work previously carried out by Burrell and Foden steam vehicles (see pages 37 and 49) was being handled by this Peerless motor lorry. Left to right: Arthur Hammond (driver), Steve Keeler, Sydney Arter. *(Christine Pope collection)*

THE 1933 Road and Rail Traffic Act imposed stringent weight limits on heavy goods vehicles — and they didn't come much heavier than steam wagons. Nearly all Bretts' steam vehicles were overweight and therefore illegal, and had to be taken off the road. Bert Brett recalled: '[The Act] completely wiped them out because they were such heavy things. The petrol people were getting rid of their Liberty lorries, which were Yankee lorries used in the First World War, and luckily we managed to get hold of a lot of those. George, our carpenter, went to work night and day, making up new bodies for them. We put them on the road as soon as we could. All that was left to do was to put a blowtorch through them [the steam wagons] for scrap. From that time the fleet was gradually built up with modern transport, from petrol to diesel.'

Bert's son, Tony, remembers the Foden wagons' last days: 'They were all lined up in 'bottom yard', smothered in grease. Grandfather hoped they would come back into their own, so he wouldn't let them rust. We children thought this was marvellous, as we had one engine each to play on, but of course we went home smothered in grease. We kept one of our Burrell Gold Medal tractors for years but eventually had to scrap it.'

Motor lorries were not entirely a novelty to the company in the 1930s — its early advertisements show that some were in service before and immediately after the First World War. By the late 1920s most of the older ones were beyond repair. For example, in 1929 a new 30 cwt Chevrolet lorry replaced an aged Garford. The firm's first modern diesel lorry pre-dated the 1933 Act: it was a 1931 AEC eight-wheel, 2,500-gallon tar tanker, which operated from Tonbridge and later from Wincheap.

The first vehicles (all of them diesels) ordered in 1933 were two AEC Mammoth Major tank wagons and an AEC Matador three-way tipper. The Matador had a Duralumin body and was Wincheap Depot's first all-metal lorry. During the next few years more tankers were acquired, among them an AEC Mammoth Major-8, Bretts now having won a contract to haul benzol, as well as tar. By 1938 the company was carrying more than seven million gallons a year for SETAR, compared with one million gallons in 1928.

The depot became exceptionally busy in 1936, with the delivery of its first Fords (three 5-cubic yard tippers and a 5 cwt van), a Leyland Octopus benzol tanker and three Leyland Beaver tippers.

From 1937 the fleet was augmented with ERF and Bedford lorries. By now the Wincheap Depot was the home of one of Kent's most modern road haulage fleets. Its flagship appears to have been Leyland JG 7213, a 5-ton 6-cwt six cylinder diesel lorry bought new in 1936. It took part in that year's Canterbury Carnival, carrying a model of the Leaning Tower of Pisa and an appropriate advertising slogan.

Several motor cars, purchased for the firm's directors and managers in the 1930s, were looked after at the depot, including a Morris 10, a Morris Major, a Morris Isis, a Ford V8 and a Humber.

Steam won a brief reprieve in 1934 when Bretts bought a new Sentinel S4 steam waggon and trailer, built from lighter components than earlier models. Veteran drivers remember it as the most stylish of all Wincheap Depot's steam vehicles. In 1940 a second-hand Sentinel was purchased from A. Jempson of Rye. When petrol was rationed during the Second World War the Sentinels enjoyed a new lease of life. Fuelled with coal from Betteshanger Colliery they delivered beer to Truman, Hanbury & Buxton's pubs in Canterbury (The Imperial, Martyrs' Field Road and The Castle, Castle Street) and Thanet, whose trade had been boosted by Kent's huge population of soldiers, sailors and airmen.

From an advertisement in the Canterbury Operatic Society's 1924 programme. This was one of Bretts' first petrol lorries and was proudly announced as being capable of travelling one hundred miles in a day. *(Canterbury Reference Library)*

A Peerless petrol lorry at 'top yard', Wincheap, with driver William ('Toby') Worrell, *c.* 1925. The vehicle delivered sand and gravel. Toby worked at Wincheap Depot from 1922 (when he was 14) until about 1929, when he joined the East Kent Road Car Company.

Driver Bill Stone (extreme right) with his mate George Savage (on the lorry) and two unidentified colleagues at Bridge *c.* 1930, with a Peerless petrol lorry on hire to George Browning's building firm. The vehicle was probably an ex-US Army truck. *(Doreen Garner collection)*

Drivers Frank Mills (left) and Horace Weatherall take a break beside a hop garden during a summer's day on the road in one of Wincheap Depot's Dennis motor lorries. The photograph was taken by George Dilnot and the back of the original print bears his handwritten caption: 'Frank and Horace, met on the road to Canterbury 3rd July 1931.' *(Audrey Gilham collection)*

Bretts' Sentinel S4 and trailer at the Sentinel Waggon Works in Shrewsbury, ready to be delivered to Wincheap Depot. It was usually driven by Albert Ades, who joined Bretts in March 1929 as a Foden wagon driver.

Bretts' entry in the 1936 Canterbury Carnival, built at Wincheap Depot and manned by (left to right) Jackie Burt, Dave Marsh and Jimmy Clarke. The lorry is Leyland JG 7213, new that year, and is parked in St Nicholas Road, Thanington. When the lorry reached Wincheap the tower had to be lowered, to pass under the two railway bridges. JG 7213 was driven by Arthur Hammond until 1957. By then it had clocked up 400,000 miles and Bretts bought Arthur a new Leyland, NFN 308.

Ford lorry JG 7910 loaded with gravel at Riverdale Road Quarry, *c.* 1937. The driver, probably Albert Weatherall, has stowed his broom and shovels and is ready to leave. Two shovels were carried; one for sand and gravel, the other for coal collected from local collieries for Bretts' steam boilers and the various stoves and fires that warmed the firm's premises.

AEC Matador JG 4111 at an unidentified location. (*Colin Smith collection*)

AEC Mammoth Major-8 JG 4112 in 1938, outside No. 16 St George's Place, Canterbury, Bretts' head office from 1934 to 1942.

'I left the handbrake off!' George Webster's Bedford (possibly JG 9032, bought in 1937) takes a nose dive at Riverdale Road Quarry. Manager Sid Burton (extreme left) and colleagues prepare to sort out the problem. *(Charles Bentley collection)*

5: Sports and outings

Cyclists and officials at Bretts' Sports Ground on Whit Monday 1937 at a Day of Sport which revived the annual Whitsun sports meetings inaugurated by George Felix Finn in 1883. William Brett and Robert Brett snr are standing second and fourth from the left. The cyclists competed in a 880 yards cycle race, won by Sally Parkinson (right) of Gravesend Cycling Club in 1 minute 26 seconds. *(Frank Bailey)*

IN the 1930s the number of employees based at Wincheap Depot grew to well over one hundred. Bretts' directors encouraged them to organise sports and social events, treated them to an annual outing, and introduced improved employment benefits — including holidays with pay. In 1934 the sports ground was restored and Bretts' Sports Club was formed. Joe Murrin, groundsman at St Lawrence Cricket Ground, Canterbury, prepared two cricket pitches, first used in 1935. A second-hand demountable building was purchased in Herne Bay for £13.10s and re-erected on the western side of the sports field, for use as a sports pavilion and clubroom. Robert Brett laid its foundation stone on November 21, 1935, and commemorated the occasion by planting a poplar tree close to the row of poplars he had planted for G.F. Finn 51 years earlier.

At a dinner on March 21, 1936, the pavilion was formally opened by William Brett, the sports club's president. The souvenir menu tells us that such delicacies as 'Roast

Gearbox and Thick Engine Oil' and 'Flints, Pebble Dashings and Tarmac in season' were enjoyed by more than one hundred members and guests. After-dinner entertainment was provided by Will Russell's concert party, and by J.W. Vissenga, who showed his cinefilms of an employees' outing in 1934 and the laying of the pavilion's foundation stone.

On Whit Monday 1937 the company revived the annual Whitsun holiday sports, which had lapsed for more than 20 years, by holding a Day of Sport in aid of Kent and Canterbury Hospital, whose new building at South Canterbury was nearing completion.

Bretts' Sports Football Club joined the first division of the Canterbury League in 1934/5 and finished at the bottom of the table, but from then on standards improved. Within a few years the club had teams in the Canterbury and District League and the Kent Amateur League. The club won the Kent Junior Cup in 1937/8, the Kent Benevolent Cup in 1938/9, came second in Division 2 of the KAL eastern section in 1938/9 and second in the KAL north region in 1939/40.

While opening the Day of Sport on Whit Monday 1939, the Mayor of Canterbury, Councillor Mrs C.E. Williamson, appealed for volunteers to become air raid wardens or join the Auxiliary Fire Service, Civil Nursing Reserve or Land Army. War was imminent, and Wincheap Depot was about to experience total upheaval.

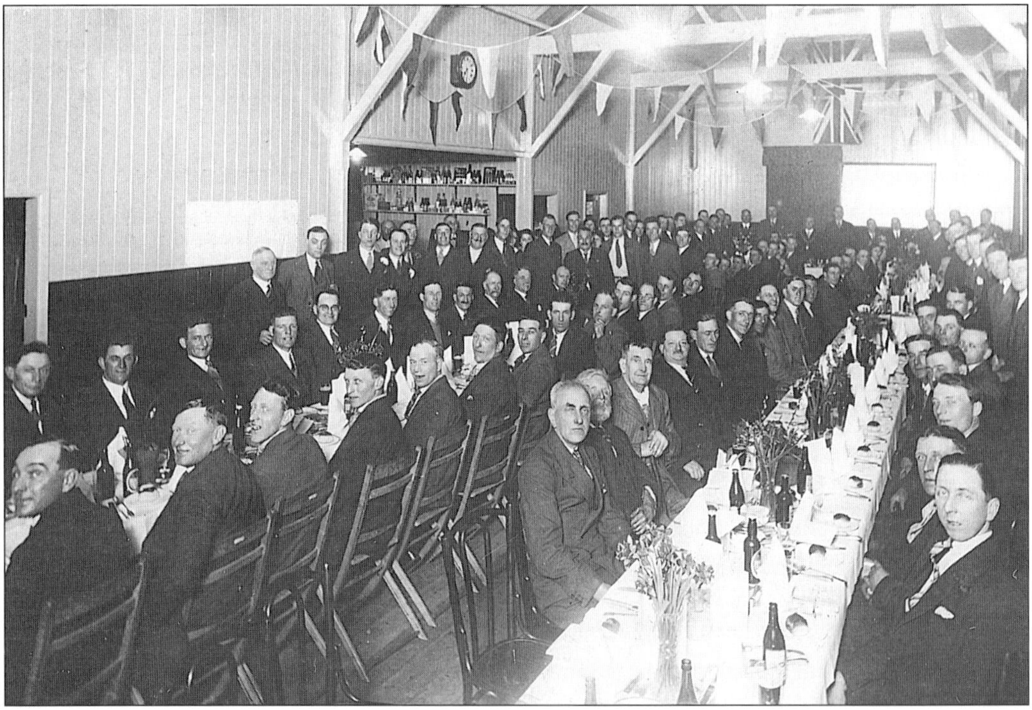

Bottled beer and bread rolls before them, employees of Robert Brett & Sons wait for their first course — 'crude tar purée' — at a dinner to mark the official opening of Bretts' Sports Club's pavilion at Wincheap in 1936. *(B.& W. Fisk-Moore)*

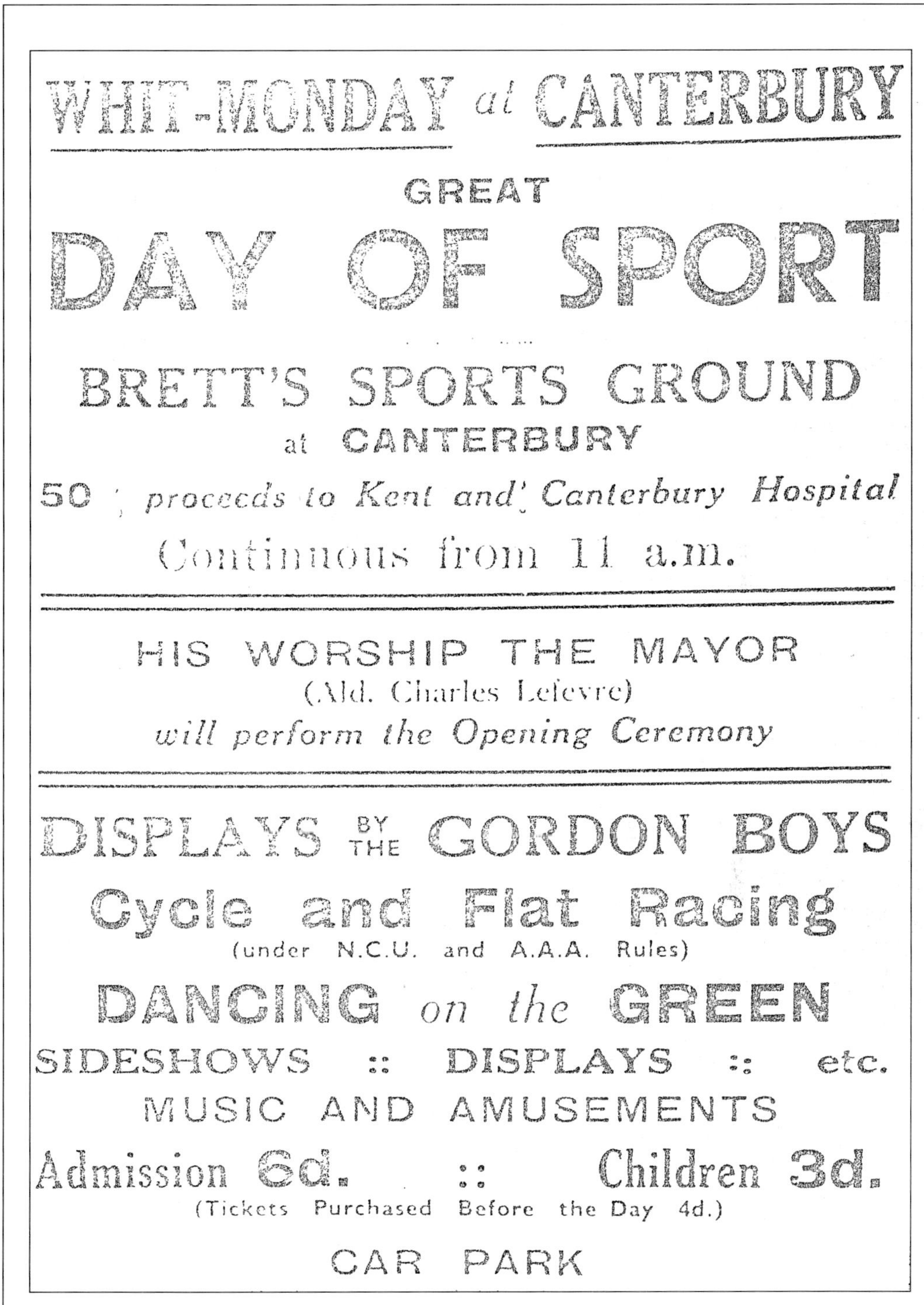

WHIT-MONDAY *at* CANTERBURY

GREAT

DAY OF SPORT

BRETT'S SPORTS GROUND

at CANTERBURY

50% *proceeds to Kent and Canterbury Hospital*

Continuous from 11 a.m.

HIS WORSHIP THE MAYOR

(Ald. Charles Lefevre)

will perform the Opening Ceremony

DISPLAYS BY THE GORDON BOYS

Cycle and Flat Racing

(under N.C.U. and A.A.A. Rules)

DANCING *on the* GREEN

SIDESHOWS :: DISPLAYS :: etc.

MUSIC AND AMUSEMENTS

Admission 6d. :: Children 3d.

(Tickets Purchased Before the Day 4d.)

CAR PARK

Only sixpence for a day out at Bretts' Sports Ground. From the Kentish Gazette, May 15, 1937.

The Mayor of Canterbury, Alderman Charles Lefevre (second from left, front row) with officials and other guests at the 1937 Day of Sport, photographed at the entrance to the sports pavilion. Other personnel identified are: front row, Mrs Lefevre, the Mayoress of Canterbury (on Ald. Lefevre's right) and Winifred Smith (hon. secretary of Bretts' Sports Club); centre row (from the left) William Brett, Percy Forwood (referee and cycling handicapper) and Stanley Ackroyd (chairman of the organising committee); back row (second from left), Les Richardson (hon. secretary of the sideshows committee. *(Frank Bailey)*

Ned Harris (right) of Gravesend Cycling Club gains a narrow lead over Harold Daniels of Canterbury Cycling Club in a four-lap race at a pre-war athletics and cycling meeting. *(Kentish Express/Harold Daniels collection)*

Dr H. Harrison, who succeeded Alderman Lefevre as Mayor of Canterbury, opens the 1938 Day of Sport. *(Frank Bailey)*

The formalities over, William Brett and other officials and guests join in the fun at the sideshows. *(Frank Bailey)*

One of the oldest surviving photographs of Brett cricketers, taken during an inter-departmental match *c.* 1935. Left to right, back row: Ted Latham, Ted Tritton, Archie Mills, Sid Burton, Jimmy Clarke and an unidentified umpire; centre row: Robert Brett jnr, William Brett, Bert Brett, Stanley Ackroyd; front: John Brett (left) and an unidentified player. Behind the team is the cricket pavilion that stood in the south-east corner of the sports ground.

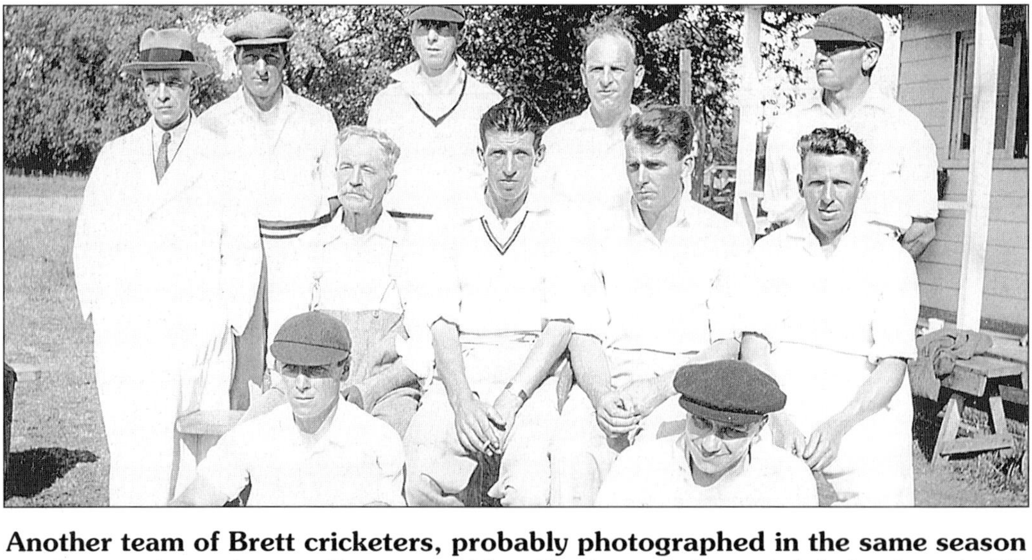

Another team of Brett cricketers, probably photographed in the same season as the previous picture. Personnel identified are (left to right), back row: (2) Norman Rye, (3) Archie Mills, (5) probably Arthur Hammond; centre row: (1) Bert Bourne, (2) Fred Rye, (3) George Weatherall, (4) Len Marsh; front: (2) Bill Knott.

Five Brett cricketers during a pre-war game at St Stephen's CC. Left to right: Jimmy Clarke (with bat and pads), Albert Keam, Stanley Ackroyd, Ted Tritton and Wally Twist (who scored 20). Mrs Twist is sitting between Ted and Wally. *(Ted Tritton collection)*

Bretts' Sports Club second XI cricketers, *c.* 1938. Left to right, back row: Horace Weatherall (umpire), Roy Coaker, Bill Longley, Jackie Burt, Wally Twist, Bill Gambell, Francis Tilly (scorer), John ('Bunny') Hare; front, Archie Mills, Doug Toze, Jimmy Clarke, Stanley Ackroyd, Ted Tritton. *(Malcolm Longley collection)*

Brett cricketers, probably playing as 'Bill Longley's XI', at Canterbury Gas & Water Company's sports field, Wincheap Grove, *c.* 1937. Left to right, back row: Ernie Hambrook, Bill Field, Bill Longley, Bill Hambrook, Ray Couchman, Jimmy Clarke, Richard Skelton; front, Les Tremlett, Jack Bickerdike, Miss Bing, Jack Tremlett, Bill Gambell. Miss Bing was scorer for Watling Street Institute and Watling Street Old Boys cricket teams. *(Malcolm Longley collection)*

At Southend during Bretts' outing in 1937. Left to right: Norman Rye, Fred Marsh, Albert Weatherall, Harry Rye, Horace Weatherall, Charlie Maple and Fred Keam. *(Barbara Tilly collection)*

Bretts' Sports Club footballers and officials in 1938. Left to right, standing: William Brett, Stanley Ackroyd, H.C. ('Sammy') Bridgeland, Bill Field, Bill Gambell, Ted Tritton, Albert Ades, Richard Skelton, Bert Brett. Centre row: Jimmy Clarke, Norman Else, Stephen Fuller (captain), Ray Couchman, Archie Mills. Front: Harry Hopkins, Ian Newing. The men in football kit were members of the team that won the Kent Junior Cup in 1937/8. 'Sammy' Bridgeland (Royal Army Ordnance Corps) died in a Japanese POW camp in the Second World War and Ray Couchman (Royal Air Force) was killed in a plane crash shortly after the war ended. *(B.& W. Fisk-Moore)*

Bretts' Sports Club's 1938/9 darts team outside the sports pavilion at Wincheap. Left to right, standing: Frank Mills, Harry Rye, Albert Keam, Archie Mills, John Ratcliff, Norman Rye, Stanley Ackroyd, Frank Smith (club steward). Sitting: Alfred (Fred) Sharp, Fred Moore, Bert Brett, Fred Rye, William Brett, Len Marsh, Horace ('Ted') Latham. *(B.& W. Fisk-Moore)*

On a pre-war outing to Brighton. Left to right, standing: Sydney Arter, Norman Rye; sitting: Albert Weatherall, Tom Sackett and Percy Sackett. *(Percy Sackett collection)*
Below: Wincheap Depot workmates and colleagues from other Brett departments on the Thames during an outing to Windsor Castle and Hampton Court, probably in 1939.

6: Wartime and afterwards

A Canterbury 'Dad's Army.' Several men from Wincheap Depot, among them Private Harry Ward, Private Tom Hatch, Corporal Bill Groombridge and Corporal George Knight, are in this picture of No. 2096 Coy. Mechanical Transport Home Guard, alongside men from other Brett departments and Canterbury firms, including Lt Frank Brett (Robert Brett's nephew) of Elgar Brett & Sons. *(B.& W. Fisk-Moore/Sylvia Wilkinson collection)*

WINCHEAP Depot did its bit in the Second World War and in post-war construction work. During anti-invasion precautions early in the war, several of the depot's lorries and drivers were posted to Army bases at Bifrons, Patrixbourne and Mystole Park, Chartham, to help haul guns into position along the defence lines. Two of Bretts' new ERFs were requisitioned by the Army, so the depot had to hire lorries in order to fulfil its contracts. The depot's drivers delivered huge quantities of sand and gravel to military construction sites, while Central Workshops' fitters worked flat-out servicing and repairing lorries and quarrying plant.

William Brett was appointed sub-district manager for the Ministry of War Transport and put in charge of commercial motor fuel rationing, assisted by his transport manager, Charles Bentley. William was also the local Home Guard's motor section transport commander.

Part of the depot became a munitions factory, making breech-loading mortars for landing craft, parts for six-pounder guns used at the Battle of El Alamein, and tracks for Valentine tanks. Thirty young women conscripts were taken on to replace men who had joined the armed forces.

Robert Brett, the company's founder, died on March 27, 1941 and William and his brother Bert took charge of the company's affairs.

The area called 'the orchard' — adjoining the sports ground, the Elham Valley Railway embankment and the rear gardens of several houses in Wincheap — became a camp for the Royal Artillery, who in February 1941 installed a mobile 18-inch gun, the 'Bochebuster,' on the railway, to bombard Kent's beaches in the event of a seaborne invasion.

On June 1, 1942 Bretts' head office at No. 16 St George's Place was totally destroyed during the Baedeker air raid. The sports pavilion at Wincheap was quickly converted into offices. 'We had to make a big effort next day, building partitions and doors,' recalled carpenter Ron Feakins. Later that summer a barrage balloon unit — one of several set up around Canterbury at this time — took over the sports ground. On October 31, while all the balloons were grounded for essential repairs, about 20 Messerschmitt 109s strafed main streets and residential areas and dropped high explosive and incendiary bombs. Several houses in the York Road area of Wincheap were destroyed.

'The blast shook down the carpenters' shop's chimney," said Ron. "It landed on top of a Ford truck. I'd only just finished rebuilding its coachwork.' This was the only damage the depot sustained throughout the war.

Thirty years later, engineering department employee John Port recalled those days: 'If there was any trouble getting the balloon down, we would hang on to the guide ropes until it was secure. In return the crew gave us early warning of enemy aircraft approaching. After a moonlighting trip around Hollow Lane they would bring in sacks of apples and cherries to share among the night shift, and we often thought we could smell chicken stew and fried eggs coming from their mess hut.'

In the summer of 1945 life at Wincheap Depot started to return to normal, as service personnel resumed their pre-war jobs and more people were taken on to cope with the huge demand for sand, gravel and transport and plant hire services. The lorry drivers, mobile plant operators and maintenance teams worked from dawn until dusk for councils and contractors who were repairing war-damaged buildings, redeveloping bombsites and building new housing estates and schools in and around Canterbury. In their makeshift head office in the sports pavilion, staff struggled to ensure that their paperwork kept pace with all that was going on in and beyond the depot. One unusual contract for Central Workshops involved refurbishing, for civilian use, a number of Army lorries which had been recovered from Singapore harbour, where they had been dumped during the Japanese invasion.

Peacetime work had to be found for the engineering factory. A Brett subsidiary company, Canterbury Precision and Engineering Works (renamed Canterbury Precision Engineers in 1966) was established in what had been the munitions factory. The Vickers Armstrong aircraft company became a good customer after a car carrying two of its engineers had a puncture outside Wincheap Depot. They called in to seek help, saw the well-equipped engineering facilities, and eventually placed contracts for the manufacture of components for airliners.

This demountable aeroplane hangar saw service in the First World War at one of Kent's aerodromes and at Wincheap Depot in the Second World War. It was purchased by Bert Brett in about 1920 and erected in 'bottom yard' to accommodate workshops for the depot. It was demolished in 1990.

Part of the pre-war and 1940's transport fleet at Sturry Quarry, *c.* 1947, photographed by Sid Burton, quarry manager. Sid Maple leads in KJ 5723, a 1932 Duralumin-bodied AEC Mammoth 8-tonner. Behind it are a wooden-bodied ERF (driver: probably Jimmy Hawkins), a 5 cu. yd capacity Bedford petrol lorry (driver: Harry Ward) and one of several ERFs (possibly JG 9407) bought in 1937 or 1938 (driver: Albert Ades or Norman Rye). In the background: the Canterbury - Margate railway.

George West with BFN 852, one of three ERF five cylinder diesel end-tippers bought in 1940 and 1941, photographed by Jimmy Hawkins near Littlebourne in the early 1950s when the lorry was out on its first run after being resprayed at Wincheap Depot. By now Bretts' lorries had fleet numbers painted on their cabs. This one was No. 61. The lorry is hauling a draw-bar trailer. These were taken out of service in the late 1950s. The lorry was fitted with a high-speed rear axle in 1958, raising its top speed from 28 mph to 33 mph. *(Jimmy Hawkins collection)*

Eleven members of Bretts' staff in 1946, outside the sports pavilion which was converted into a temporary head office in 1942. Left to right, standing: Basil Pearman, Ted Tritton, Norman Else, Charles Bentley, Jack Kinnear, George Weatherall; sitting: Beta Daly, Muriel Spicer, Margaret Hollis, Miss Moody, Jimmy Rathbone. *(Ted Tritton collection)*

William Brett reviews his 'troops' as they wait in 'top yard' on September 28, 1946 for coaches to take Bretts' staff on their first post-war outing, to a variety show at the London Palladium. Staff identified are Evelyn Smith, Audrey Mangold, Alice Groom, Evelyn Brice and Winifred Smith (nos 10, 11, 12, 14 and 20 from the left in the front row), John Wyborn (second from left on lorry) and Norman Hayward (looking to his left over Evelyn Brice's right shoulder).

Forties fashions on parade during the 1946 outing, as Vernon Kirby enjoys a beer and a smoke. Other personnel identified are (left to right): (1) and (2) the Tremlett sisters, (3) Winifred Smith, (4) Muriel Spicer, (7) Margaret Hollis, (12) Mary Smith, (13) Molly Lawrence, (14) Evelyn Smith.

Cost office staff on the sports ground in 1947. Left to right: Vera Jacobs, Pat Cole, Jean Baldock, Evelyn Brice, Audrey Mangold. *(Audrey Ryn collection)*

Clockwise, from bottom left: glimpses of the tyre shop, workshops and vehicles at Wincheap Depot, 1947. In the first three pictures Alice Groom (now Alice Falkner) is on the left, with Audrey Mangold (now Audrey Ryn). In the fourth picture they are with an unidentified friend. *(Alice Falkner collection)*

William Brett's 1937 Humber in 'top yard' in 1947, after it had been washed and polished by chauffeur Tom Sackett. *(Brian Sackett collection)*

Wincheap Depot's transport fleet and drivers on the sports ground in 1948. Drivers identified are Don Rogers (far right), Harold Hoare, Steve Keeler, Fred Gipps and Albert Jarvis (third, fourth, fifth and 11th from the right) and Horace Weatherall (in front of fifth lorry from the left). The intrusion must have worried groundsman Bill Longley, but as it is midsummer and the ground is dry, the wheels caused little or no damage to the cricket outfield.

No other vehicles in sight as ERF lorry DJG 439, hauling a mobile crane on an ex-Army low loader, waits outside 'top yard.' The lorry's regular driver was Norman ('Pud'ney') Rye, who has probably called at the depot to ask transport foreman John Ratcliff, 'Where do you want me to take this little lot?'

Another coachload of employees ready to set off on the 1948 outing. This picture was taken at about the same time as the one on page 4. Personnel identified standing in the road are (from the left): (3) George Fassum, (5) Fred Warwick, (6) Mrs Bird, (7) Vernon Kirby, (8) Charles Bentley, (10) Bill Knott. In the coach, Doug Toze looks out of the open window on the far left and Archie Stokes looks out of the one on the far right. In the door, Sid Burton peeps over the shoulder of the man wearing the cap.

En route to London in 1948. Personnel identified are (left to right): (1) Beta Daly, (2) Margaret Hollis, (4) Ken Lawrence, (5) Winifred Smith, (6) Jimmy Clarke, (7) Miss Attwood, (8) Muriel Spicer, (9) Bert Andrews, (10) Ted Tritton, (12) Fred Tritton, (13) George Weatherall, (14) 'Dizzy' Stoakes, (15) Mrs Bird, (17) Vernon Kirby, (18) Charles Bentley and (19) Ted Wadsworth — an ex-Quartermaster Sergeant known as 'Q' to his colleagues.

Dinner time for employees before returning to Canterbury after the 1948 outing. The man closest to the camera is John Ratcliff. Personnel identified in the row facing John are (from the left): (2) Harry Rye, (4) Fred Marsh, (5) Wally Twist, (6) Sam Brown, (7) Dick Fedarb. Second table, back to camera: (4) Bill Horne jnr (behind Fred Marsh); facing camera (from the right): (2) Percy Sackett, (3) Albert Weatherall, (4) George West. *(Percy Sackett collection)*

ERF lorry DJG 439 from Wincheap Depot hauling a steam rail crane from Riverdale Road Quarry, Canterbury, to Sturry Quarry, *c.* 1948. Driver Norman Rye has just turned into Fordwich Road from Water Lane, Sturry. George Hudd, the crane's operator, watches from his bicycle. The other onlooker is Norman's mate, Don Martin.

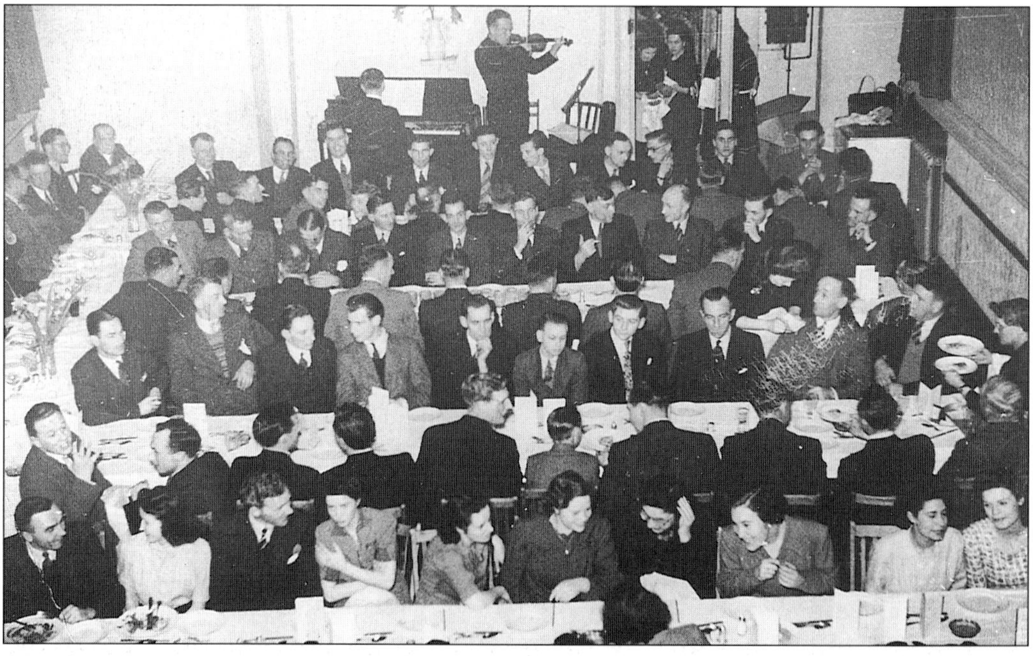

Employees from Wincheap Depot, head office and other departments are serenaded by a violinist at the company's first post-war dinner, held at Canterbury's Talisman Restaurant on February 2, 1949.

An ERF lorry driven by Norman Rye, towing a Ruston Bucyrus 19-RB crane on a low loader, gets hitched to Leyland JG 7213, driven by Arthur Hammond, outside the East Kent Sessions House in Longport, Canterbury, in the mid-1950s. 'Double headers' like this were needed to haul heavy loads up St Martin's Hill.

A 1938 ERF lorry, AFN 401, driven by Don Rogers delivers bricks (probably Shelford sand-lime bricks) to the builders of Canterbury's new bus station in 1956. Photographed from St George's Terrace. *(Kentish Gazette/Nigel Tilly collection)*

Driver Fred Rye watches as his Bedford lorry is loaded with Blitz rubble by a 19-RB excavator clearing the site for Canterbury's Longmarket shopping centre in January 1958. *(Kentish Gazette)*

Rubble, bricks, gravel, snow — you name it, Wincheap Depot's team shifted it. This WWII Caterpillar tractor, driven by Jimmy Hawkins or Cyril West, is at work on the A253 near Monkton, Thanet, after a blizzard in the 1950s. Peter Spratt, retired mobile plant fitter, recalls many hazardous journeys along country lanes to reach snowploughs that had broken down in conditions like those shown here. *(Tim Keenan/Tony Blake collections)*

7: Carnivals and family fun

Sylvia Sackett (17), Canterbury's Carnival Queen and her Maids of Honour, Betty Danton (16) and Patricia Sedgwick (19), enthroned on a Brett lorry at the head of the Canterbury Carnival parade on August 6, 1953. *(Kentish Gazette)*

AFTER the war, groundsman Bill Longley repaired six years of wear, tear and neglect at the sports ground and created a greensward comparable to St Lawrence Cricket Ground, where he learned his craft before the war. Bretts' cricket and soccer teams were reformed, and employees at Wincheap Depot teamed-up with colleagues from other departments to support local events, such as the annual Canterbury Carnival. In 1953, when Sylvia Sackett was the city's Carnival Queen, she rode in the procession on a Brett lorry decorated by her father Bert, the depot's tyre fitter. The 1960 carnival gave the transport department a chance to show off its latest combo, a Leyland Beaver tractor, UJG 663, hauling a York low loader.

Events at the sports ground provided happy distractions from post-war austerity. On Whit Monday 1948 a City Sports and Gala organized by Canterbury City FC Supporters' Club attracted more than 8,000 spectators. William Brett donated two trophies: a Perpetual Challenge Cup for cycle racing and a Perpetual Challenge

Shield for inter-schools athletics. They were won by Ronald Cheeseman of Canterbury Cycling Club (who came first in the one-mile scratch race) and Sturry County Modern Secondary girls' team, which won the inter-schools relay race.

By 1949 Bretts had 260 employees — twice as many as in 1939. In July 1950 they and their families enjoyed the first of a series of annual sports days at Bretts' Sports Ground.

In 1955, when St Lawrence House, in Canterbury's New Dover Road, became the company's head office, the sports pavilion reverted to its original use and was soon a popular venue for the firm's leisure activities, and for events organised by other local companies and clubs. Bretts' Sports Club became Bretts' Sports and Social Club and in 1958 regained the full, year-round use of the sports ground, after Canterbury City FC moved to Kingsmead Stadium.

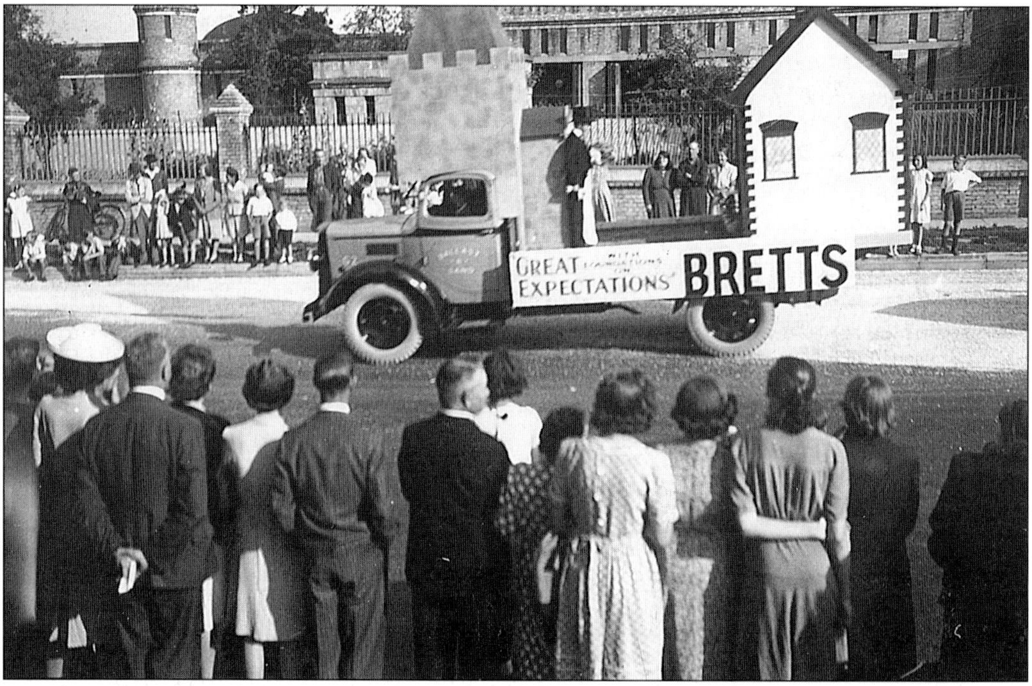

Bretts' entry, mounted on a Ford lorry (fleet no. 62), passing Canterbury Waterworks and Wincheap Depot in the 1947 Canterbury Carnival parade from Thanington to the King's School playing fields in St Stephen's Road, via all the city's main thoroughfares. The 'bride and groom' are Bunty and Roger Snell.

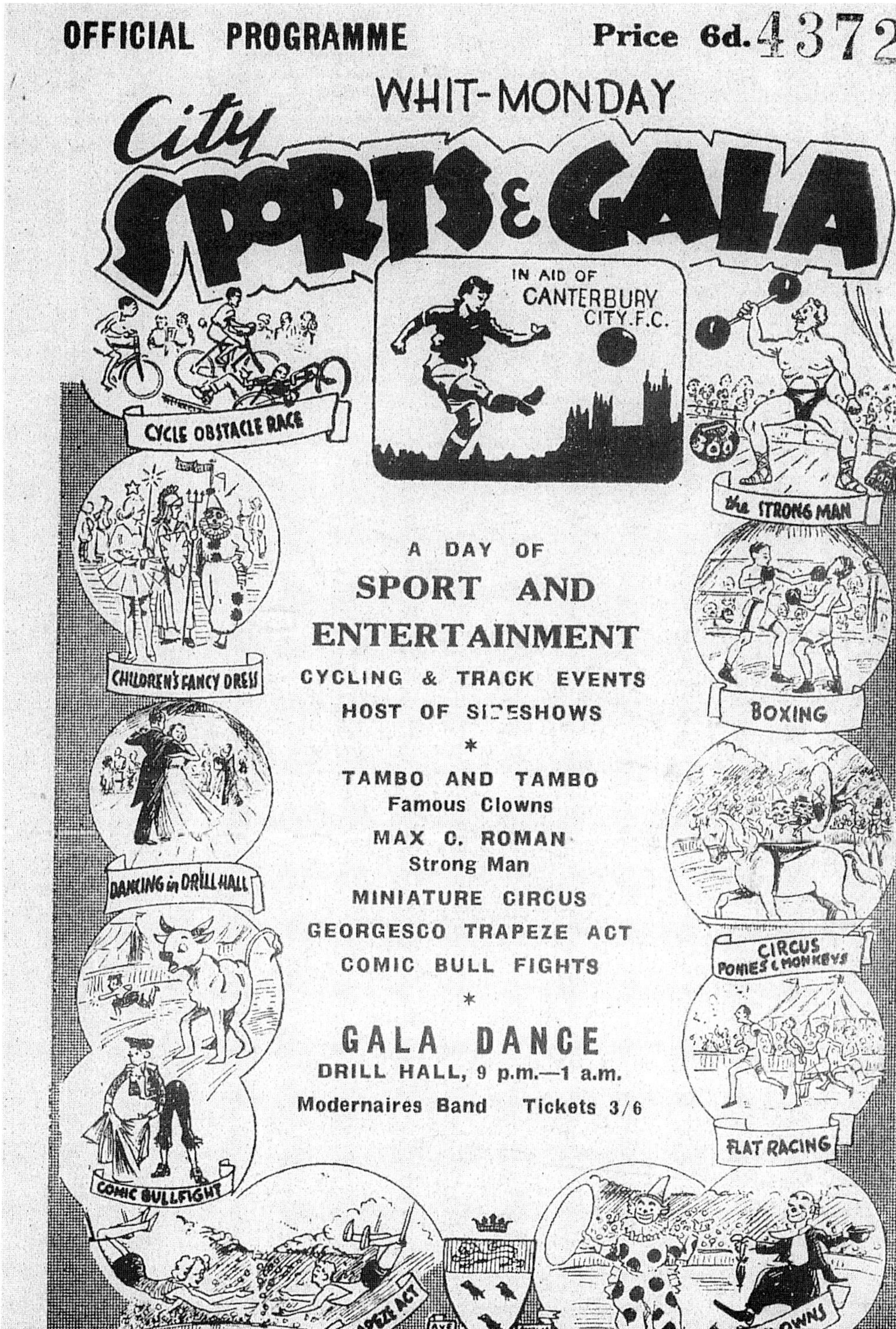
OFFICIAL PROGRAMME
Price 6d. 4372
WHIT-MONDAY
City
SPORTS & GALA
IN AID OF
CANTERBURY
CITY F.C.
CYCLE OBSTACLE RACE
the STRONG MAN
CHILDREN'S FANCY DRESS
A DAY OF
SPORT AND
ENTERTAINMENT
CYCLING & TRACK EVENTS
HOST OF SIDESHOWS
*
TAMBO AND TAMBO
Famous Clowns
MAX C. ROMAN
Strong Man
MINIATURE CIRCUS
GEORGESCO TRAPEZE ACT
COMIC BULL FIGHTS
*
GALA DANCE
DRILL HALL, 9 p.m.—1 a.m.
Modernaires Band Tickets 3/6
BOXING
DANCING in DRILL HALL
CIRCUS
PONIES & MONKEYS
FLAT RACING
COMIC BULLFIGHT
TRAPEZE ACT
AVE
MATER
ANGLIA
CLOWNS

PLAN of the SPORTS & GALA ARENA, TRACK AND SIDESHOWS

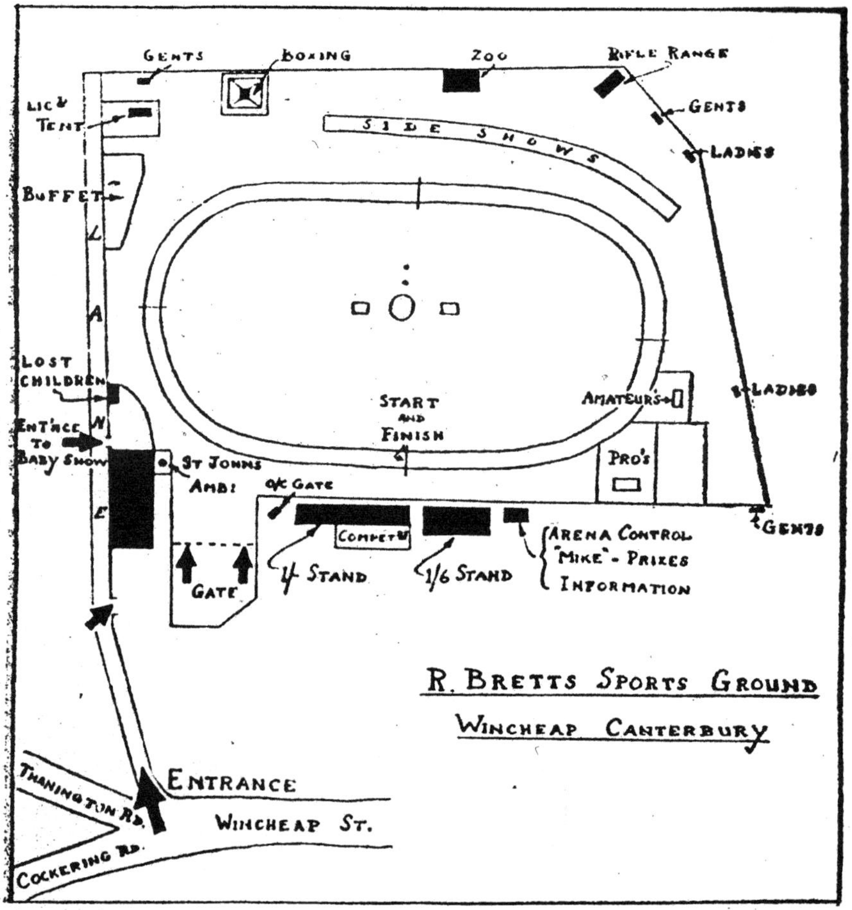

- Continuous Programme of Attractions on the field from 11.30 a.m.-7.30 p.m.
- Refreshment Tent (by Slatters). Running Buffet all day.
- Licensed Bar by Mr. F. Hart, Hop Poles, Wincheap.
- St. John Ambulance Brigade in attendance under Superintendent A. E. Shelley.
- Baby Minding and Lost Children's Tent. (See Plan.)
- Adequate Parking Arrangements.
- The Ground is served by Buses Nos. 1, 2, 22, 24, 27, 67.
- All Enquiries to Committee Tent. (See Plan.)
- Loudspeaker Arrangements.
- **DON'T FORGET THE GALA DANCE, DRILL HALL, 9 p.m.—1 a.m.**

The Modernaires Dance Band

From the programme for the 1948 City Sports and Gala. *(David Elliott collection)*

Florence Brett presents the Brett shield to the winners of the inter-schools relay race at the 1948 City Sports and Gala. Left to right: Ann Mann, Winifred Holliday, Barbara Morgan and Marie Sullivan.

Ronald Cheeseman, winner of the Brett cup, with (from the left) Peter Philpott and Douglas Griggs of the Canterbury Cycling Club and Florence Brett.

The starter - identified as George Weatherall or Sid Burton - at the 1950 sports day.

Mums and office girls get into their stride. In the background: Canterbury City FC's grandstand and terraces and, behind the grandstand, one of Bretts' workshops.

A close finish in the 75 yards race for girls aged 9 -12. Result: (1) B. Ward, (2) S. Spice, (3) D. Edwards. In the background: the sports pavilion and Bretts' technical laboratory. In the distance: Thanington housing estate.

The 60 yards race for girls aged 9 and under. Result: (1) W. Wilkinson, (2) A. Snell, (3) N. Matcham. Among the adults immediately behind the girls are (from the left) Arthur Hammond, Ted Tritton and John Port (with the two clowns). At the megaphone: Tom Walkeden.

'On your marks!' Among the athletes of varying abilities on the starting line are (from the left): Jack Martin (1), John Port (2), George Webster (4) and Doug Toze (8). In the background: the wartime Army building that became the footballers' changing rooms. Among the spectators standing behind the runners are Albert Jarvis (wearing cap, facing right), Percy Sackett (facing camera) and Albert Weatherall (standing on Percy's left).

'Bite the apple without using your hands.' Roger Snell (third from right), Paul Tritton (far right) and four unidentified competitors in the obstacle race. Result: (1) J. Franklyn, (2) R. Snell, (3) B. Ward.

Among the couples identified in this three-legged race are (from the left) (1) Ted and Mary Tritton, (3) George and Doreen Webster, (5) Jack Anderson and May Edwards.

'I know how to boil one, but this is ridiculous!'

'One more heave!' Transport drivers winning the tug-o'-war. Personnel identified are (from right to left): (1) Arthur Hammond, (2) Bill Groombridge, (3) George Webster, (4) Jimmy Hawkins, (5) George Knight and (6) Tom Hatch. In the background: the cricket pavilion and buildings in the area known as 'the orchard.'

Watching the fun from their deckchairs in front of the grandstand. Left to right: (1) and (2) Robert Brett jnr and his wife Beatrice, (3) Florence Brett, (4) Bert Brett, (5) William Brett, (6) Irene Kinnear, (7) Jack Kinnear, (8) Clare Snell, (9) Valerie Kinnear.

'Cowboy Ken' Stokes and Canterbury City FC soccer fan Wendy Wilkinson at the fancy dress competition. Wendy is armed with her rattle and holding a programme for City's fixture with Snowdown, played on February 11, 1950.

All the winners. Left to right: Paul Wadsworth ('strong man'), Gillian Warwick ('strawberry'), Patricia Cox ('Channel swimmer'), Sandra Matcham ('Victorian lady'), Norma Matcham ('Tyrolean girl'), Pauline Groombridge ('Football Pools'), Wendy Wilkinson, Ann Warwick ('Hawaiian girl'), Susan Knott ('Oranges and lemons') and Kenneth Stokes. *(Sue Knott collection)*

'We're *jester* couple of clowns!' Ken Todd (right) and an unidentified work-mate.

Tiny tots and adventurous boys amuse themselves in the fairground.

Albert Ades, who drove Bretts' Sentinel steam waggon in the 1930s, applies his skills to a somewhat smaller steam engine. His passengers are (left to right), Mick Fry, Bill Stone and Jack Arter.

After the grown-ups had their ride, the children were allowed to get on board! *(Sue Knott collection)*

'Staff Ladies', winners of the bat and trap competition.

Dora Bentley finds herself seatless in a game of musical chairs, watched by referees Doug Toze (right) and Tom Walkeden. Ian Newing (far left) and Jack Anderson (wearing sunglasses) watch the fun from a safe distance.

Dazzled by the setting sun, children and parents enjoy a Punch and Judy show in front of the sports pavilion.

At a tea party and dance in the lorry garage, William Brett thanks the organisers and promises that there will be another family sports day next year.

Race marshal Tom Walkeden calls for order at the 1951 family sports day.

The boys' race. Five sprinters make for the finishing line, while on the left 'he who hesitates' probably came last. In the background (beyond the pollarded trees): Thanington Allotment Gardens.

'Shoo!' shouts Tom Walkeden, starting the little girls' race. Competitors identified are (from the left): (2) Sue Knott and (4) Linda Newing. *(Sue Knott collection)*

The race for 12 - 15 year old girls. Patricia Sackett toes the line in the far lane, watched by her mother Dorothy and brother Chris. In the background: Bretts' garage and one of the firm's lorries; an almost empty car park (most people walked, cycled or caught a bus when travelling around Canterbury in the Fifties); swings and a roundabout; and Bretts' canteen and water tower.

Toeing the line at the start of the three-legged race.

A variety of racing techniques and fashions in the ladies' race.

More egg-and-spoonery. Among the competitors are Margaret Pearson (left lane), Barbara Sackett (lane five) and Dorothy Sackett (lane six). Among the spectators behind the starting line are Margo Burton and Audrey Tindall (in the summer frock and cardigan).

Margo Burton evidently had a good day at the races. She is seen here receiving a prize from Florence Brett.

Muriel Clarke bats for Staff Ladies in the final of the inter-departmental bat and trap competition, won by Sturry Quarry.

Happy losers. Left to right: Margaret Pearson, Miss Attwood, Sylvia Geldard, Mrs Edwards, Muriel Clarke, Mrs James, Gisela Gibbons, Eileen Stokes.

Bert Brett takes aim as he and his brother William enjoy a quiet game of darts.

As in 1950, railway rides were a popular attraction. Les Todd is the driver; the diesel locomotive is from one of Bretts' quarries; the wagons were borrowed from one of Kent's collieries.

Fancy dressers on parade, including P. Wadsworth ('What Britian Kneads More Dough' [sic]), Brian Sackett ('ballet dancer'), S. Bubb ('Festival of Britain'), Patricia Cox ('Mrs Mop'), Janice and Linda Newing ('Dick Whittington and his Cat'), S. Skelton ('Chinaman') and W. Wilkinson (another 'Festival of Britain' entry).

Linda and Janice Newing (seen as 'Dick Whittington and his cat' on the previous page) receive one of the fancy dress competition's prizes from Florence Brett, as Jack Snell and Winifred Smith look on.

At the tea party, held between the afternoon and evening sports events, Jack Snell thanks Bretts' directors for a splendid day, commenting: 'This is a family business which takes a very real interest in the family life of its members.'

The 'Tower of Pisa' tableau of 1936 (seen on page 60), re-enacted at the 1960 Canterbury Carnival. Rather the worse for wear after 30 years on a workshop wall, this picture was taken in Reed Avenue and shows (left to right) Bert ('Mac') Carter, Colin Smith, Dennis Young, Jimmy Hacker, Dave Lewis and Bert Sackett. *(Colin Smith collection)*

A topical cricket theme for Bretts' entry in the 1961 Canterbury Carnival. Left to right: Bernard Miles, Colin Smith, Richard Skelton, Bert ('Mac') Carter, Martin Shaxted, Michael Skelton, John Hatch, Doug Toze, Jean Auchin, Jimmy Hacker, Bert Sackett and an unidentified colleague. *(Kentish Gazette/Colin Smith collection)*

8: Parties and pantomimes

Children of Brett employees wait at the sports pavilion on January 9, 1960 for the coaches that will take them to a pantomime at Ramsgate. A week earlier the firm had entertained their younger brothers, sisters and friends at a Christmas party at the County Hotel, Canterbury. *(Kentish Gazette)*

IN the 1950s and 1960s, parties, pantomime outings, dinners, dances and informal get-togethers were the main features of the social life enjoyed by Wincheap Depot's employees and their families. By now Bretts had so many employees that the sports pavilion could no longer accommodate large functions and bigger venues had to be hired. One of the most popular events of the early 1950s was Bretts' Sports and Social Club's Coronation dinner at the Garrison Theatre (now the Canterbury Sports Centre).

Christmas parties for employees' children were held in the ballroom at Canterbury's County Hotel but the King's Hall, Herne Bay, was the only venue near Canterbury that could accommodate the most memorable function in Bretts' post-war history — its Golden Jubilee Dinner on Saturday, October 9, 1954. The celebrations concluded with the presentation of long-service awards to 20 employees who had worked for the company for 25 or more years.

In 1959 the sports and social club, which now had 150 members, celebrated its 25th anniversary with a dinner and dance at the County Hotel. Presentations were made to two retiring officials — Ken Lawrence (36 years' service) and Albert Jarvis (20 years). D.F. Andrews proposed a toast to the club and said that with the sports pavilion back in normal service, members were now organising billiards, snooker and darts competitions.

Children whose parents worked at Wincheap Depot, head office and other Brett departments, at the firm's Christmas party on January 3, 1953.

Bretts' Sports and Social Club's Coronation dinner at the Garrison Theatre in May 1953. *(Kentish Gazette)*

One hundred and forty children aged 5 - 14 attended this party at the County Hotel on December 28, 1953. The event was organised by Jack Snell and Winifred Smith and the children were entertained by Will Russell, conjurer and ventriloquist. *(Kentish Gazette)*

Christmas

1953

At this greatest Festive Season of the year we are pleased with the opportunity it gives us to record our thanks and appreciation for the splendid consistent good work shown by all members of our organisation, which has resulted in bringing to conclusion a most satisfactory year's work.

With the passing of time our family has considerably increased in numbers, but it will be our personal endeavour to see that the family spirit which we cherish so much is well protected and maintained.

During 1954 we shall be commemorating our Jubilee. It was on February 7th, 1904, that our father, the late Mr. Robert Brett laid the foundation of this present business. We do not expect however, to celebrate on that day, but details will be given you later of the celebration which we hope will be worthy of the occasion.

Plans are well in hand for the Children's Christmas Party which takes place at the County Hotel on Monday, the 28th December, and with Will Russell in attendance we are all looking forward to a very happy time.

May we close with wishing you a really Happy Christmas, with good health and success in the New Year.

For and on behalf of

ROBERT BRETT & SONS, LTD.,
Wm. Brett, Chairman and Managing Director.
H. S. Brett, Deputy Chairman and Director.

Employees, their spouses and (at the top table) directors and guests at Bretts' Golden Jubilee Dinner on October 9, 1954. *(Kentish Gazette)*

Bill Knott of Central Workshops receives a wrist watch from Florence Brett to mark his 29 years' service. Also in the picture are William Brett (standing) and Gabriel Hews, proprietor and editor of Kent County Newspapers. *(Kentish Gazette)*

A pearl necklace for Winifred Smith, for 28 years' service. *(Kentish Gazette)*

A typical scene at one of Bretts' Christmas socials at the sports pavilion. Workshops colleagues Peter Spratt (right) and Ron Feakins are enjoying a pint. With them are their wives Gladys and Jean. A queue has formed at the bar. Later there will be a raffle, and Ted Scott will play the piano for a sing-song. *(Ron and Jean Feakins collection)*

Bretts' Christmas party on January 15, 1955, attended by 130 children. Will Russell, standing by the window with William Brett and Jack Snell, was on duty again. The party was organised by Winifred Smith and Hilda Lilley. *(Kentish Gazette).*

January 7, 1956. For some, their first Brett party. For others, their second, third or fourth. E. Wilson and A. Raven entertained with ventriloquism, conjuring and puppets. Joan Cox, May Edwards, Hilda Lilley and Winifred Smith were the organisers. *(Kentish Gazette)*

Happy and pensive moments at the parties on January 5, 1957 (top picture) and January 4, 1958. *(Kentish Gazette)*

Party time again on January 3, 1959, when Hilda Lilley and Winifred Smith organised a programme of games and competitions. David Hallett presented a conjuring and puppet show. *(Kentish Gazette)*

Albert Jarvis (left) receives a retirement gift from William Brett at Bretts' Sports and Social Club's 25th anniversary dinner. *(Kentish Gazette)*

'Under eights' are entertained by conjurer L. Allen at the Christmas party on January 7, 1961, organised by John Brett. *(Kentish Gazette)*

Later that month, two coachloads of older children prepare to set off on their pantomime outing. *(Kentish Gazette)*

Party time and an outing to a circus at Olympia in January 1962. *(Kentish Gazette).*

John Hoddinott keeps the children in order as they wait for an Underground train while on their way to a pantomime at the London Palladium in December 1962. *(Kentish Gazette).*

Members and guests at Bretts' Sports and Social Club's dinner dance at the Chiesman Pavilion, St Lawrence Cricket Ground, Canterbury, on June 6, 1980. *(Kentish Gazette)*

9: 'Up the City'

Outside left Len Dolding scores the first of Margate's three goals against Canterbury City in the 1954 Kent League Cup Final at Bretts' Corner. Dolding's header left goalkeeper Eddie Bird (behind Dolding) and centre half Harry Oliver each assuming that the other would make the clearance effort. The other players in the picture are Peter Vandepeer (Margate) and John Richards (City). *(Kentish Gazette)*

BRETTS' Sports FC was reformed for the 1946/7 season. The winter's blizzards and sub-zero weather brought the firm's quarries and transport fleet virtually to a standstill. Unable to wash their lorries on Saturday mornings, Wincheap Depot's drivers helped the footballers clear snow from the pitch, ensuring that they played all their home fixtures even though other grounds in the area remained closed for weeks. On February 1, 1947, the first XI beat Hythe 5-3 in the Section A final of the Kent Junior Cup but lost to Folkestone Reserves in a later round. The club disbanded at the end of the season and the sports ground became the home of Canterbury City Football Club, formed on the initiative of the Mayor of Canterbury, Alderman Evelyn Hews, and run by a board of directors headed by William Brett, one of the club's founders.

City played its first home match on August 28, 1947. A typical first XI line-up in the club's first season was Peters; Bishop, Fulwood or Strowger; Pattison, Gawler,

Hamilton; Heckley, Summerfield, Tutt, Scott and Small.

Despite steel rationing, enough girders, stanchions and roofing sheets were acquired to build a grandstand (opened on January 24, 1948) opposite the half-way line, flanked by covered terraces with seats and standing room. Robert Brett's poplar tree, planted nearly 13 years earlier, was flourishing on the site of one of the terraces and was allowed to grow to its full height through a hole in the roof, becoming one of Wincheap's landmarks. Behind this terrace there was an ex-Army building containing changing rooms and baths for the home and visiting teams. The ground had a floodlit training area — one of the first of its kind in Kent.

Thousands gathered at what became known to soccer fans as 'Bretts' Corner' to watch the 30 or so Kent League matches and cup ties played there every season. The biggest-ever 'gate' was on October 9, 1948, when 4,998 people watched City play Dover. Admission charges were sixpence for boys and girls, one shilling for adults. For another 'tanner' or 'bob' the game could be watched from a seat in the terrace or the front rows of the grandstand; the back rows were reserved for season ticket holders and club officials.

We City supporters sported green and white scarves and at exciting moments in the game whirled our rattles and shouted our battle cries — 'Up the City' and 'Set 'em alight, City.' When nothing much was happening we stamped our feet, blew into our cupped hands and muttered 'Come on my City lads' and 'Come on the green and whites.' Whenever the ball was kicked sky-high off the pitch we yelled 'Chatham!' This derisory exclamation harked back to a match some 50 years earlier, when Chatham played Sheppey United for a league championship. Chatham gained the lead and wasted time until the final whistle by persistently kicking the ball out of play.

Ernie Webster, who had been player-manager for Bretts' Sports FC, was City's first manager and coach and created one of the most successful teams in the Kent League. He retired at the end of the 1951/52 season. Billy Walsh was the club's player manager for the 1952/53 season and was succeeded by Bill Higgins, Jackie Henderson acting as temporary manager for a few months until Bill took up his appointment.

Many international and FA First Division stars played at Bretts' Corner, including Bill Hughes (Spurs and Wales), T. Brolly (Millwall and Ireland) and Derek Ufton and S. O'Linn (Charlton Athletic) who came to Canterbury as members of an All Stars XI that played a Combined City XI in Ernie's testimonial match on April 30, 1952. Result: 3-3. At the end of the 1952/3 season, in a benefit match for City players Phil Pattison and Denis Newstead, City lost 3-1 to a Stars XI that included Laurie Scott (ex-Arsenal and England right back), B. Brown (goalkeeper for Pegasus and England's amateur international team) and Fulham wingers Charlie Mitten (formerly of Manchester United) and A. Stevens. Charlton Athletic's First Division team played a Kent League XI in a benefit match for Kent and England cricketer Godfrey Evans.

The most exciting match at Bretts' Corner took place on May 1, 1954, when a crowd of 4,605 saw City and Margate draw 3-3 in the Kent League Cup Final. Margate won the replay 5-0. City played its last game at Bretts' Corner on May 2, 1958 and next season moved to its new home ground at Kingsmead Stadium, joining the Metropolitan League and later the Southern League. When City left Bretts' Corner, Bretts' Sports FC was reformed, playing in the Kent Amateur League and the Kent League. The club won the Kent League Cup in 1967/68 and the Kent League championship in 1968/69. In 1970 Bretts' Sports FC appointed a professional player-manager, Bobby Harrison, as successor to Peter Vandepeer, and became a professional club. The sports ground was used by the company's team and for various local junior and senior soccer competitions until 1994, when it closed pending redevelopment. Bretts' Sports FC was disbanded at the end of the 1972/3 season but reformed in 1987.

In the last soccer match at Bretts' Corner, in April 1994, Bretts' Sports FC beat Reeves & Neylan 7-3 to clinch promotion to division three of the Jewson Whitstable and Herne Bay League. The team now plays its home matches at Thanington recreation ground. Robert Brett & Sons continues to support soccer by sponsoring local teams and competitions.

Bretts' Sports FC's post-war first XI, manager and trainer on a snow-covered Bretts' Corner on February 1, 1947. Left to right, standing: Ernie Webster (manager), Doug Royel, John Hare, Richard Skelton, Harry Ward, Allen, Ron Gawler, Hadlow; sitting, John ('Buck') Ryan, Griffiths, Frank Tutt, Tom Ward, Bert Richardson. *(Kent Messenger/Richard Skelton collection)*

Canterbury City FC's first XI at an away match in the 1948/9 season, with manager Ernie Webster (left) and trainer Billy Banks. *(Kentish Gazette/Lilian Inge collection)*

City's first XI in the goalmouth at the Thanington end in November 1949, at a match at which they beat Folkestone 2-0. Left to right, back row: Len Scott (inside left), Ron Bishop (right back), George Barron (goalkeeper), Jimmy Hunter (centre half), Phil Patterson (right half); front row: Tommy O'Neil (inside right), Tommy Hopper (right wing), Wilf Heathcote (centre forward), Billy Hamilton, captain (left half), John Ryan (left wing), Ron ('Pedlar') Palmer (left back). *(David Swain collection)*

Tim Brett keeps a hand on a football autographed by Manchester United — first prize in a raffle at Ernie Webster's testimonial match. Standing on Tim's left at the table are Kent cricketers Fred Ridgeway and Godfrey Evans, who helped sell the tickets. *(Kentish Gazette)*

An exciting moment at the Thanington end as Sheppey United goalkeeper Matthews makes a dramatic save during a Kent League match on February 28, 1953. City won 2-0. *(Kentish Gazette)*

One of City's three goals against Folkestone Town in a Kent League match at Bretts' Corner on September 19, 1953. City won 3-2. *(Kentish Gazette)*

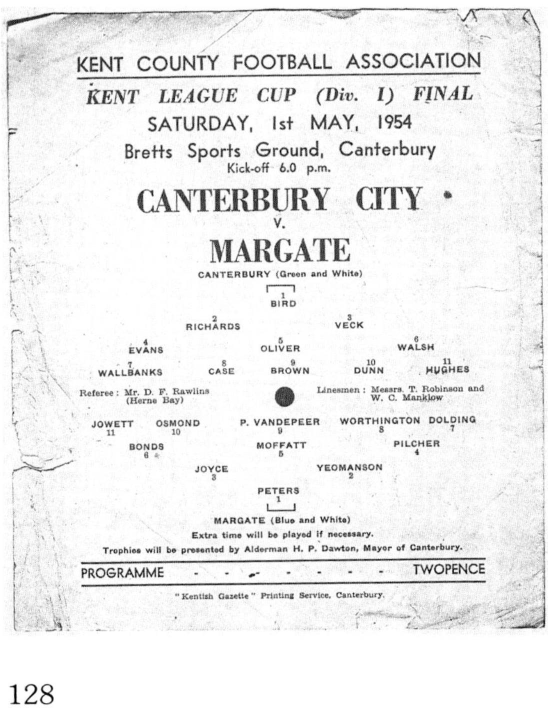

KENT COUNTY FOOTBALL ASSOCIATION

KENT LEAGUE CUP (Div. I) FINAL

SATURDAY, 1st MAY, 1954

Bretts Sports Ground, Canterbury

Kick-off 6.0 p.m.

CANTERBURY CITY

v.

MARGATE

CANTERBURY (Green and White)

1 BIRD

2 RICHARDS 3 VECK

4 EVANS 5 OLIVER 6 WALSH

7 WALLBANKS 8 CASE 9 BROWN 10 DUNN 11 HUGHES

Referee: Mr. D. F. Rawlins (Herne Bay)

Linesmen: Messrs. T. Robinson and W. C. Manklow

JOWETT 11 OSMOND 10 P. VANDEPEER 9 WORTHINGTON 8 DOLDING 7

BONDS 6 MOFFATT 5 PILCHER 4

JOYCE 3 YEOMANSON 2

PETERS 1

MARGATE (Blue and White)

Extra time will be played if necessary.

Trophies will be presented by Alderman H. P. Dawton, Mayor of Canterbury.

PROGRAMME - - - - - - - - TWOPENCE

"Kentish Gazette" Printing Service, Canterbury.

From the 1954 Cup Final programme. *(David Elliott collection)*

Canterbury City FC's players, directors and committee members in front of the grandstand in 1955. Personnel identified are (from the left), back row: (2) Bob Morley, (3) probably John Richardson, (4) Henry Brown, (6) Tom Francis, (7) Bill Higgins, (8) Bob Hawkins, (9) 'Pip' Skinner, (10) Mick Marsh, (11) Willie Craig, (13) Jack Henderson, (14) Bill Banks; second row: (1) Bob Veck, (2) Roy Evans, (3) Alf Woodcock, (4) Ted Tritton, (5) Gabriel Hews, (6) Jack Snell (chairman), (7) S.H. Loxton, (8) Stanley Jennings, (9) F. Butcher, (10) R. Kent, (11) Charles Bates, (12) Les Stevens, (13) Norman Hooper; front row: (1) Tony Dunn, (3) Willie Brown, (4) Alan Danton, (5) George Pope, (6) Arthur Nugent, (8) John McIvor. *(Kentish Gazette/Ted Tritton collection)*

One of Bretts' Sports FC's 1960s teams and club officials at Bretts' Corner. Personnel indentified are (from the left), standing: (1) John Brett (chairman), (2) Charlie King, (3) Malcolm Longley, (4) Richard Skelton, (6) Bert Prett, (8) Henry Dale, (9) John Williams; sitting: (3) Ernie Bradshaw, (5) Michael Longley. *(Kent Messenger/Malcolm Longley and Richard Skelton collections)*

Bretts' Sports FC's first XI on March 23, 1963. Left to right, back row: W. Higgins (manager), E. Bradshaw, A. Dewell, J. Williams, D. Rigden, C. Troth, C. Williams, E. Shakespeare (trainer). Front: M. Holmes, D. Roy, J. Roy, D. Goldsack, J. Phipps, A. Danton. Photographed on Deal Town's ground, where they lost 3-2 to Margate Athletic in the final of the Kent Junior Cup (Eastern Section). *(Kentish Gazette)*

Bretts' Sports FC's Kent Amateur League squad at Bretts' Corner in May 1967. Players and officials identified are (from the left), standing: (1) Robert Scott, (2) John Brown, (3) David Jeffreys, (4) David Roy, (5) Alan Gawler, (6) Ron Gawler, (7) David Rigden, (8) Peter Stroud, (9) Colin Goldsack, (10) Roland Mansfield, (11) Roy Hood, (12) Roy Baker; sitting: (1) John Baker, (2) John Phipps, (3) Vic Redpath, (4) Peter Vandepeer, (5) John Brett (chairman), (6) Eric Shakespeare, (7) Ken Blissett. *(Kentish Gazette)*

St Augustine-Canterbury Schools XI at Bretts' Corner on October 26, 1968, before beating Bromley-Beckenham Schools 12-0 in the second qualifying round of the English Schools Trophy. The members of the St Augustine-Canterbury Schools team were: Paul Hornibrook (Technical), Brian Jemmett (Faversham), Clive Hawkins (Simon Langton), Freddie Beer (Archbishop's), David Hendrie (St Anselm's), John Colnutt (Sheerness), Paul Wisdom (Technical), Gary Diggery (Sturry), Kevin Giles (Archbishop's), Neil Howell (Sir William Nottidge), Malcolm Daniels (Technical); reserves, Paul Iwass (St Anselm's), Martin Christie (Archbishop's). *(Kentish Gazette)*

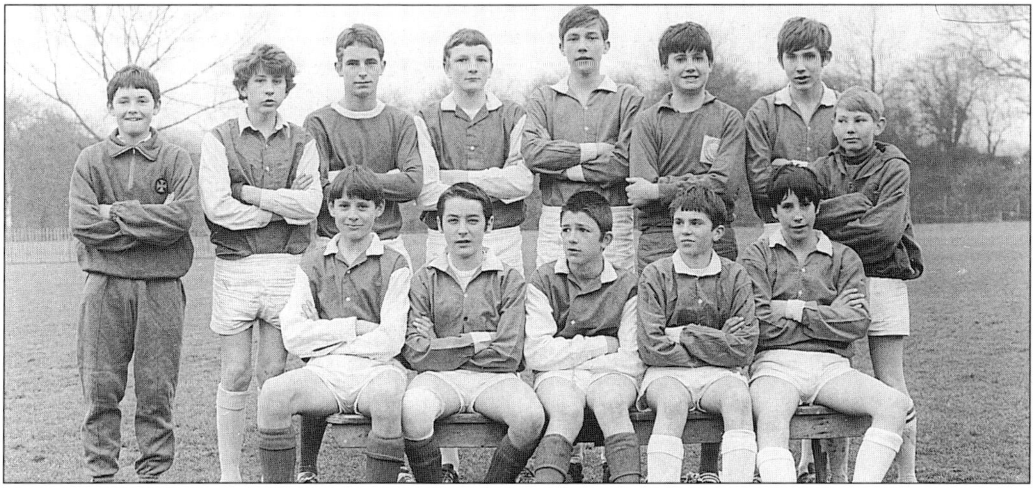

Technical High School's team, which won the St Augustine-Canterbury Schools' third year soccer championship at Bretts' Corner on March 25, 1969, beating Archbishop's 11-0. Left to right, standing: Julien Turrell, David Gilham, Gary Hopper, Michael Kolsek, Steven Huggins, Robert Blackwell, Chris Urwin, David Marsh; sitting: Peter Rothermal, Owen Davies, John Rush, Graham Roberts, Roger Surginson.

Archbishop's, losers in the 1969 schools' soccer championship. Left to right, standing: Kevin Scott, Andrew Waller, Melvin Snow, Clive Wainwright, Timothy Epps, David Pilbeam, Timothy Kendall, Christopher Beaumont; sitting: Malcolm Constable, Graham Epps, Nigel Minter, Geoffrey Garrad, Martin Curd. *(Kentish Gazette)*

The Bretts' Sports team that won the Kent League Championship by beating Deal Town Reserves 3-1 at Bretts' Corner on May 10, 1969. Left to right, standing: Ron Simpson, Peter Brooks, Colin Tomlin, Dave Manning, Bobby Pearce, Trevor Pearce, David Roy; sitting: Peter Caples, Dennis Parkin, Charlie Prescott, Ken Blissett, David Bright. *(Kentish Gazette)*

North East Kent Boys, one of the schoolboy teams that played at Bretts' Corner in the 1950s and 1960s. This one lost 5-1 to Medway Towns in the first leg of the final tie for the President's Shield. Left to right, standing: Steane (Technical), Jeffrey (St Dunstan's), Longley (St Dunstan's), Friend (Sturry), Millen (Technical), Mills (Simon Langton); sitting: Williams (Technical), Edwards (St Dunstan's), James (St Dunstan's), Preston (Technical), Brian Wanstall (Whitstable). *(Kent Messenger/Malcolm Longley collection)*

All except the ref keep their eyes on the ball during an incident on January 17, 1970, when Bretts' Sports FC held Canterbury City to a 1-1 draw in a Kent Senior Cup match at Bretts' Corner. Bretts lost the replay at Kingsmead Stadium 2-1. *(Kentish Gazette)*

Bretts' Sports FC, losers 0-2 at home to Bexhill Town in an FA Cup tie at Bretts' Corner on September 25, 1970. Left to right, back row: Graham Dawson, Ian Plant, Colin Tomlin, Barry Beaney, Reg Goreham, Denis Parkin, John Hamblin; front: Bob Pearce, Roy Laker, Glen Dempsey, Gordon Burden, David Bright. *(Kentish Gazette)*

John Brett, chairman of Bretts' Sports FC, with Wincheap Sports and Kennington 'A' and 'B' — three of 50 teams that took part in a five-a-side soccer tournament at Bretts' Corner in 1972. Kennington B beat Wincheap 5-4 in the final. *(Kentish Gazette)*

An angry scene in front of the grandstand during Bretts' Sports FC's Kent Senior Cup tie with Margate on December 30, 1972. Result: 2-2. Margate won the replay 1-0. *(Kentish Gazette)*

Bretts' Sports FC in 1987, when the team was reformed to play in the Herne Bay and Whitstable Sunday League. Left to right, back row: David Petts, John Swanborough, Mark Davey, Simon Woods, Graham Gallant, Craig Taylor, Steve Hewitt; front: Chris Welch, Gary Laker, Neil Amos, Richard Harvey, Keith Cooper, Steve Millard.

Bretts' Sports FC's 1994/95 team. Left to right, back row: Paul Davey, Rudy Gilham, Brian Chatfield, Stewart Haynes, Mick Knight, Mark Davey, Gary Pittman, Sheldon Fagg; front, Mark Chatfield, Andy Twyman, Steve Terry, Allen Terry, Mark Goke. The team was photographed after beating Faversham Royals in the Catling Cup final. *(Mark Davey collection)*

The last football photocall at Wincheap. Thanington FC's under-nines squad in May 1995 in new kit donated by Bretts. Left to right, back row: Alan Turner (trainer), Tim Brett (chairman, Robert Brett & Sons Ltd), Graham Williams (team manager); centre row: Mat Fassett, Christopher Williams, Liam Tuite, Darren Bushell, Dean Bushell, Philip Murray, Wilfred Meaden, Owen Baker, Lee Hollingsbee; front row: Richard Murray, Jason Tutt, Wayne Giles, Dominic Evans, Daniel Newport. *(Kentish Gazette)*

10: Vintage cricket

An early post-war Bretts' Sports cricket team outside the cricket pavilion at Bretts' Sports Ground. Personnel identified are (from the left), back row: (1) Ray Marsh (umpire), (2) Jack Snell, (3) Ted Tritton, (4) Norman Else, (5) Arthur Hammond, (6) Bill Longley, (7) Sid Burton; sitting: (2) Ian Newing, (3) Richard Skelton (wicket keeper), (4) Fred Tritton, (5) Jimmy Clarke. *(Ian Newing collection)*

FOR nearly 60 years, playing or watching cricket at Bretts' Sports Ground was one of life's simple pleasures. Spectators who tended to doze the game away set up their deckchairs beside the picket fence in front of the sports pavilion, taking advantage of the shade offered by the ash tree that flourished near the gate leading on to the field. Most of us, though, gathered around the cricket club's own pavilion, near the railway bank. On the verandah, one or two small boys who had volunteered to help the scorers would be clanking around, constantly shuffling and replacing the numbered tin plates on the scoreboard.

The ground was a delight to play on — a favourite among club cricketers from all over Kent — but it had one disconcerting characteristic. Fielders staggering backwards to take a lofty catch on the boundary would suddenly notice that the ground beneath their boots seemed to have become hollow: this was because they were running across the turf-covered cinders of the cycle track. Some of the players' wives and girlfriends missed the spectacular catches and sixes that enlivened nearly every game: they were over in the main pavilion, preparing the teas. After the match the bar would open and the home team would treat the visitors to a round of drinks.

For 36 years the sports ground was immaculately maintained by Bill Longley, who was also a useful No. 3 batsman for Bretts' Sports CC. On June 18, 1949, on his home ground, he scored 100 not out (including 15 fours) during a second wicket stand of 103 with Doug Toze (43) in a match against Nonington. Doug's unbeaten 143 against Beverley on June 30, 1956 was probably the highest score by any player at the sports ground. The scorebooks for 1948 - 1964 — one of Bretts' Sports vintage eras — record several other centuries by Doug, including 138 against Norfolk and Suffolk Nomads in 1963 and 106 n.o., 122 n.o. and 105 against Dover Cosmopolitan in 1954, 1955 and 1962. In 1962 he also scored 102 n.o. against Beverley and 117 n.o. against Tenterden.

In the 1954 match against Dover Cosmopolitan, Doug and Alan Shaxted (68) put on 150 for the first wicket. The fixtures with the Dover team usually inspired fine batting. In June 1952 Doug (54 n.o.) and Alan (46 n.o.) gave Bretts, the home side, a 10 wicket win; in a return match Alan made 112 of Bretts' 241 for 3 declared in a match that Cosmopolitan managed to draw. Gore Court's visits to the sports ground brought out the best in Alan — 107 n.o. in a six wicket victory in 1954 and 124 n.o. in a drawn match in 1955. Norman Else (102 against Westgate on Sea in 1948 and 108 n.o. against Herne Bay in 1961) was another batsman whose arrival at the crease always created a buzz of excitement. Not that big scores were inevitable. A week after soundly beating Norfolk and Suffolk Nomads, Bretts' Sports were all out for 42 against Hythe, losing by 7 wickets.

On Coronation Day in 1953 William Brett and his son John captained opposing twelve-a-side teams. William was now 60 years old and this was probably his last game. His team made 134 for 9 declared but John's side won by 8 wickets, thanks largely to 79 n.o. by Doug Toze. While walking up Wincheap on our way to the match, some of us lingered at Southwood's shop window and marvelled at being able to see some of the Coronation proceedings 'live' on television.

At the end of the 1953 season Bretts' Sports Cricket Club held its first annual dinner. Gabriel Hews, proprietor of Kent County Newspapers, presented the 'Kentish Gazette cricket bat', autographed by Kent and England wicket keeper Godfrey Evans, to Alan Shaxted — his prize for being the best batsman in junior cricket during the second half of the season. Alan had been runner-up in a similar competition in the first half of the season; his average for the season was nearly 70.

Bretts' Sports had occasional fixtures with a John Brett XI. In 1960 John's team knocked up 141 for 2, thanks to an opening stand of 116 by John (52) and his brother Tim (71 n.o.). The club team replied with 101 for 7. In the following year's match, Bretts' Sports declared at 191 for 7 (A. Shaxted 89 n.o.), only to be beaten by six wickets (Tim Brett 120 n.o., D. Martin 31).

The last cricket match at Bretts' Sports Ground took place on September 10, 1994. Bretts' Sports scored 207 for 5 in 42 overs. Their opponents, Old Hartsdonians, were 115 for 4 when the match was rained-off. The team disbanded in 1995. Robert Brett & Sons continues to support cricket by sponsoring the Brett Canterbury District League, in which 16 East Kent teams compete for the Brett Cup.

Bretts' Sports CC's first XI in 1950. Left to right, standing: Richard Skelton, Eric Hughes, Ron Gawler, Maurice Shaxted, Alan Shaxted, John Wyborn, Alf Foster (umpire); sitting: Arthur Hammond, Ron Feakins, Brenda Hammond (scorer), Ian Newing, Doug Toze, Jimmy Clarke. *(Entwistle Photographic Services/Ian Newing and Richard Skelton collections)*

The first XI in 1953. Left to right, back row: Jimmy Clarke, Maurice Shaxted, Stan Collingwood, Ron Gawler, Eric Hughes, Arthur ('Ted') Galvin (umpire); centre row: Arthur Baker, Ian Newing, Roy Evans; front row: Alan Shaxted, Richard Skelton, Doug Toze. *(Ian Newing collection)*

Bretts' Sports CC's annual dinner at the County Hotel on September 26, 1953. *(Kentish Gazette)*

Twenty three cricketers — two teams and a reserve? - at Bretts' Sports Ground when Bretts' Sports CC played John Brett's XI on September 12, 1959. Personnel indentified are (from the left), standing: (1) Ray Marsh (umpire), (2) Les Abel, (3) Geoff Stickells, (6) Ron Gawler, (7) Malcolm Longley, (8) Alan Edwards, (9) Ernie Bradshaw, (10) Charlie King, (11) Maurice Shaxted, (12) Arthur Galvin (umpire); sitting: (5) John Williams (and his son), (6) John Brett, (7) Alan Shaxted, (8) Ian Newing, (9) Richard Skelton, (10) Doug Toze, (11) Michael Holcombe; front row, Norman Else, Linda Newing, Alan Shaxted's son Martin. Result: Bretts' Sports, 186 for 6 dec. (A. Shaxted 79), John Brett's team, 154 for 4 (N. Else 66). *(Kent Messenger/Malcolm Longley collection)*

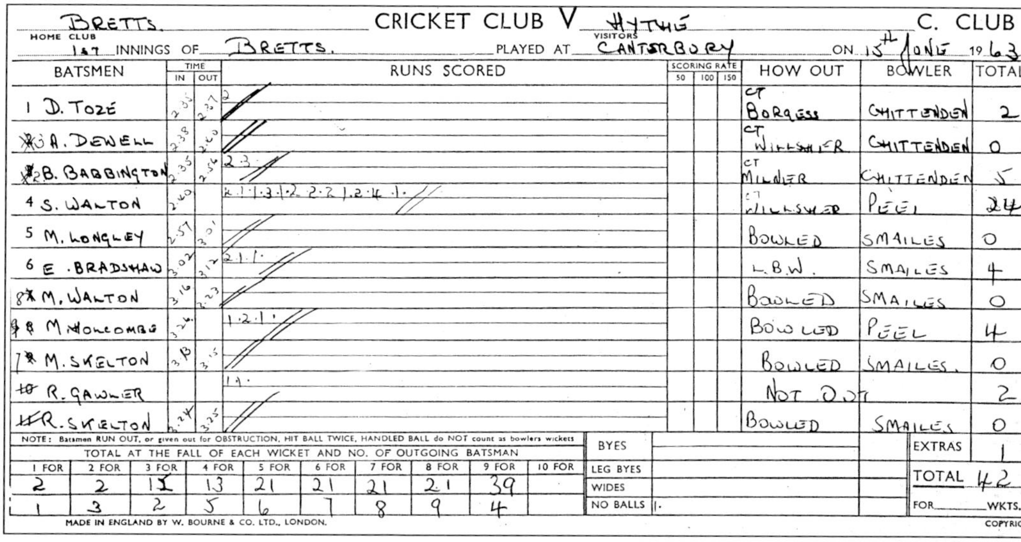

BRETTS. CRICKET CLUB V HYTHE C. CLUB
HOME CLUB / VISITORS
1st INNINGS OF BRETTS. PLAYED AT CANTERBURY ON 15th JUNE 1963

BATSMEN	TIME IN	TIME OUT	RUNS SCORED	HOW OUT	BOWLER	TOTAL
1 D. TOZE	2.35	2.37	2	CT BORGESS	CHITTENDEN	2
3 A. DEWELL	2.38	2.40		CT WILLSHIER	CHITTENDEN	0
2 B. BABBINGTON	2.35	2.56	2.3	CT MILNER	CHITTENDEN	5
4 S. WALTON	2.40		2.1.1.3.1.2.2.2.1.2.4.1.	CT WILLSHIER	PEEL	24
5 M. LONGLEY	2.57	3.01		BOWLED	SMAILES	0
6 E. BRADSHAW	3.02	3.12	2.1.1.	L.B.W.	SMAILES	4
8 M. WALTON	3.16	3.23		BOWLED	SMAILES	0
9 M. HOLCOMBE	3.24		1.2.1.	BOWLED	PEEL	4
7 M. SKELTON	3.13	3.15		BOWLED	SMAILES	0
10 R. GAWLER			1.1.	NOT OUT		2
11 R. SKELTON	3.24	3.25		BOWLED	SMAILES	0

NOTE: Batsmen RUN OUT, or given out for OBSTRUCTION, HIT BALL TWICE, HANDLED BALL do NOT count as bowlers wickets

TOTAL AT THE FALL OF EACH WICKET AND NO. OF OUTGOING BATSMAN

1 FOR	2 FOR	3 FOR	4 FOR	5 FOR	6 FOR	7 FOR	8 FOR	9 FOR	10 FOR
2	2	11	13	21	21	21	21	39	
1	3	2	5	6	7	8	9	4	

BYES	
LEG BYES	
WIDES	
NO BALLS	1.
EXTRAS	1
TOTAL	42
FOR ___ WKTS.	

MADE IN ENGLAND BY W. BOURNE & CO. LTD., LONDON. COPYRIGH

All out for 42 - and but for Stan Walton's 24 the scorer would have had even less to do in this match at Bretts' Sports Ground in 1963.

Bretts' Sports CC in 1972. Players identified are (from the left), back row: (2) David Stringer, (3) Paul Thomas, (4) Bernard Hackney, (5) Steve Bryant; sitting: (1) Ernie Bradshaw, (2) John Brett, (4) David Holness. *(Kentish Gazette)*

Bretts' Sports CC in 1981. Left to right, back row: Alan McLean, S. Pledge, Stan Walton, Ian Farquhar, Mark Vinten, Peter Fowkes, Mark Delo; sitting: David Holness, Bernard Hackney, Simon Fowler (with Bryan Davies), Mike Davies, John Rose. *(Kentish Gazette/Peter Fowkes collection)*

Bretts' Sports Ground in the summer of 1982, from the boundary of the cricket field. Photographed from about the same viewpoint as the pictures on pages 11, 19-23 and 34. *(Kentish Gazette)*

11: More sports ground memories

Teddy Ford keeps the youngsters company in the fairground at Bretts' Sports and Social Club's flower and vegetable show and fête on July 13, 1967. *(Kentish Gazette)*

SOCCER and cricket matches were the main events at Bretts' Sports Ground but other sports, including archery, bat and trap, cycle racing, rifle shooting and tennis, were also enthusiastically supported. Fêtes were among the other summertime attractions, and in winter the sports pavilion was a venue for darts, fencing, pool, indoor shooting and table tennis. Eventually, the pavilion had to be enlarged to cope with the ever-increasing numbers who came to these events and to the club's social functions; the extension was officially opened in May 1976 by Kent and England cricketer Les Ames.

With William Brett as its president, Canterbury Cycling Club flourished in the 1950s and the sports ground became its home track. Competitors cycled from as far away as Ashford to take part in league and cup events, which continued there until the late 1960s. The cyclists used the passenger shelter at the bus stop opposite the lane leading to the sports ground as the starting and finishing point for their time-trials along the A28.

For about 30 years the sports ground was a venue for archery tournaments, one of which — the 23rd William Somner Tournament on September 3, 1978 — attracted more than 200 competitors from all over southern England.

In April 1962, Battle of Britain ace Wing Commander Stanford Tuck opened Bretts' Rifle Club. 'Shooting is something which requires very great precision,' he wheezed through clouds of black gunsmoke, after firing a few shots which only grazed the target. 'The club is going great guns,' said John Brett, the club's chairman. In 1965 an outdoor range was opened on the sports ground and shooting became an all-year-round activity. In 1972 the club became the Brett and Canterbury Rifle Club.

In October 1956 the pavilion was hired by the Amateur Fencing Association and the Kent County Amateur Fencing Union for Canterbury's first weekend fencing school, instructed by Professor A. Mallard and Professor K. Russell. Two months later, at a time when the Olympic Games had revived interest in fencing, the pavilion was the venue for the Whitstable Fencing Club's first knock-out competitions. Mrs I. Mallard donated a handsome trophy to the winner.

Keenly contested darts championships and informal games were enjoyed in the sports pavilion. In summer, company and local league teams played bat and trap on the cricket outfield. Bretts' bat and trap tradition is maintained by a team which plays in the Canterbury and District Ladies' League.

For a week in June 1979 the sports ground had a garden party atmosphere, as Bretts celebrated its 75th anniversary. Customers and civic and community leaders were entertained in a marquee near the sports pavilion and enjoyed a marching display by the Band of the Royal Marines, Deal.

Bretts' Sports and Social Club's archery tournament in 1954. Competitors and spectators identified are (from the left): (1) Bert Sackett, (3) Eric Hughes, (6) Mary Tritton, (7) Christopher Tritton, (8) Ted Tritton, (9) Tom Walkeden, (10) William Brett, (11) Jack Martin (who won the 1954 and 1955 tournaments), (14) Rosemary Sackett, (15) Bertha Sackett, (16) Rita Gipps, (17) Bill Gipps, (18) Paul Tritton, (19) Peter Newport.

John Hambrook of Canterbury Cycling Club winning the William Brett Perpetual Challenge Trophy during one of the cycling championships at the sports ground in the 1950s. Peter Kingsford is in second place. *(John Hambrook collection)*

A Tuesday evening Kent Track Racing League meeting in the 1950s. The cyclists are (left to right) Jim Kennett, Phil McFarlane, John Clifford, M. Weaver, R. Abel and an unidentified rider. Joe Moyes, the starter, is on the left. Joe Amos (wearing cap), former captain of Canterbury Cycling Club, watches from the trackside. John Hambrook (wearing the dark jacket) trots along behind Kennett. *(John Hambrook collection)*

Beneath shields spelling out Bretts' name, fencing enthusiasts receive instruction during the Kent County Amateur Fencing Union's course at the sports pavilion on October 5 and 6, 1956. *(Kentish Gazette)*

A Kent Track Racing League event on June 4, 1957. The cyclists at the starting line are (from the left) Roly Crayford, Roy Manser, Dick Wallis and possibly Brian Large (all members of San Fairy Ann CC), Arthur Pursey (Medway RC) and Maurice Weaver (Faversham C & AC). The starter is Arthur Wright of Canterbury Cycling Club. Alan Aldridge of San Fairy Ann CC, seen here steadying Roly Crayford, was the evening's star performer, winning the three mile race and the 12-lap prize. *(Kentish Gazette)*

Winners of indoor shooting trophies in 1965. Left to right, standing: Henry Dale, Frank Stickings (Kent Small Bore Rifle Association), John Brett, John Port; sitting: Sid Dalton, Janet Perkins. *(Kentish Gazette)*

Wing Commander Stanford Tuck (centre), team captain John Port (right) and Reg Beasley, Bretts' Sports and Social Club's secretary, take aim at the official opening of Bretts' Rifle Club in April 1962. Among the spectators are (from the left): (1) Henry Dale, (2) Tom Walkeden, (3) John Brett, (10) Hugh March, (11) Liz Ovenden and (12) Ken Ovenden. *(Kentish Gazette)*

Not quite how it was done in Sherwood Forest. The Sheriff of Canterbury, Councillor Mary Rothermel, shoots the first arrow to open Canterbury Archers' new season on March 30, 1969. *(Kentish Gazette)*

Caroline Marshall (wearing the crocheted hat) finds a bargain at a fête held during Bretts' Sports' five-a-side soccer tournament in 1971, won by Waverley Wanderers. A touch of glamour was added to the occasion when members of the Marlowe Theatre's cast of Dames at Sea attended the official opening, accompanied by the theatre's manager, Peter Carpenter. *(Kentish Gazette)*

On the merry-go-round at Canterbury Conservatives' annual fête on June 29, 1975. *(Kentish Gazette)*

Shooting-trophy winners at the Brett and Canterbury Rifle Club's annual dinner on April 28, 1973. Left to right: B. Johnson, J. Broadley, R. Lacey, Diana Millard, K. Overrill, D. Smith, A. J. Walkenden. *(Kentish Gazette)*

'Oh my poor back!' Les Ames unveils a commemorative stone after opening the extension to the sports pavilion on May 4, 1976. *(Kentish Gazette)*

Canterbury Precision Engineers' darts team, winner of Bretts' inter-company darts league in 1977. John Brett presents the trophy to team captain Dave Taylor during a darts evening at the sports pavilion. *(Kentish Gazette)*

Tim Gutsell of Long Bridge Youth Club demonstrates his skills on Bretts' Sports and Social Club's new pool table in April 1978. *(Kentish Gazette)*

One of the teams of Cub Scouts that took part in tug-o'-war and It's a Knockout competitions before a crowd of 2,000 at Canterbury, Whitstable and Herne Bay District Scout Council's 'Midsummer Madness' fête in 1978. *(Kentish Gazette)*

Archery action at the William Somner Tournament on September 3, 1978. Opened by Lady Paramount, the shoot comprised a York round for men, a Hereford round for ladies and a Western round for juniors and higher-handicapped adults. The champions were: T. Ransom (York), Mrs P. East (Hereford), Miss J. Davis and D. Hart (Western). *(Kentish Gazette)*

Contestants in the Canterbury and District Ladies' Bat and Trap League's singles championship in July 1982. Players identified are (from the left): (1) Joan Gower, (2) Grace Delo, (4) Shirley Kyle, (5) Molly Hudson, (6) Shirley Chaney, (8) Daphne Macender, (10) Sandra Carey, (15) Ann Evans, (16) Janet Whittaker. Janet, of Mill House, won the championship by beating Avril Child of Dolphin A. *(Kentish Gazette)*

Tim Brett, chairman of Robert Brett & Sons, addresses guests at the company's 75th anniversary luncheon, held in a marquee on the sports ground on June 20, 1979. At the top table are (from the left), A. Pilcher (Furley Page Fielding & Pembrook), Rodney Hews (chairman, Canterbury Magistrates), Dr S.J. Cox (chairman, Kent County Council), Margaret Brett, Councillor and Mrs W.A. Wildman (Deputy Mayor and Mayoress of Canterbury), L.J.C. Stockwell (Sheriff of Canterbury) and Mrs Stockwell.

A marching display by the Band of the Royal Marines, Deal, during the 75th anniversary celebrations.

Barely a lifetime after primitive hot air balloons first ascended from the sports ground, helicopters were making occasional appearances there — as on this occasion in February 1981, when some of Bretts' managers flew to JCB's factory at Uttoxeter. *(George Weatherall).*

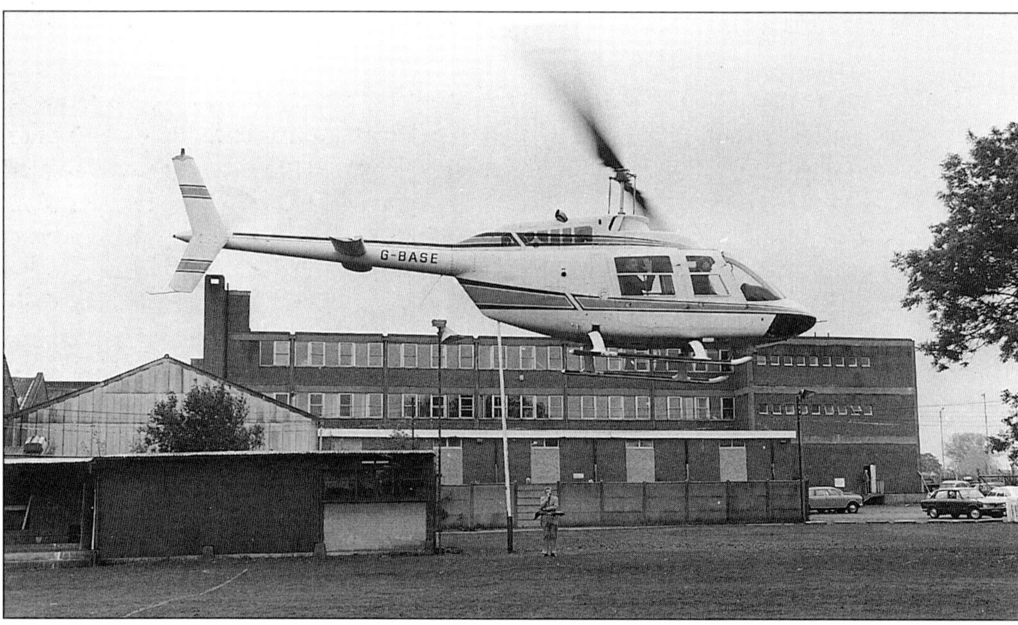

Executives from the National Coal Board's Minestone Executive depart after a meeting with Brett directors in October 1981. *(Kentish Gazette).*

12: On the lorries

Norman Rye (right), driver of Wincheap Depot's Leyland Beaver tractor, and 'Chuckles' Ford prepare to haul a traction engine from Holman Bros. yard in Dover Street, Canterbury in 1964, on the first stage of its journey to a private collector in Herne Bay. In the background, Bretts' ex-Army Bedford QL recovery truck which had helped load the engine.

WINCHEAP Depot's workshops and its road haulage and mobile plant fleets were expanded and modernised in the late 1950s and 1960s, after many years of 'make do and mend' necessitated by post-war economies. The delivery of a Leyland Beaver tractor type 14 B10 and an articulated York low loader to Brett Plant Hire in May 1960 heralded a new era in haulage and plant hire services; heavy loads would now be towed on 'artics' instead of on draw-bar trailers and wagons. The Beaver, registration number UJG 663, fleet number 136, became a familiar sight in and around Canterbury, towing cranes and other huge loads to quarries and building sites.

On a smaller scale, the purchase of a Whitlock Dinkum Digger in 1958 was another significant step forward. It was the firm's first wheel-mounted mobile excavator and easily driven from site to site — unlike its track-mounted predecessors, which had to be hauled on low loaders when travelling more than a mile or two. Bernard Miles from Central Workshops was responsible for on-site repairs to the Dinkum. In 1964 the hire fleet received its first wheel-mounted mobile crane, an 11-RB. The cab went to where it was needed under its own power; its jib followed on a lorry.

The transport fleet also acquired a modern image as sleeker tipper trucks replaced models which were beginning to show their age, and whose working lives had been extended time and again thanks to the skills of the Central Workshops' team. The new lorries, with their heaters, self-starters, wide windscreens and other comforts, were envied by retired drivers, who remembered when even a windscreen was considered to be a luxury!

By-passes, dual-carriageways and motorways removed most of the notorious traffic pinch-points that the drivers had contended with. Another change was the disappearance of some of their long-established transport cafés, where they could buy a cup of tea for tuppence and, if the proprietor didn't object, eat the sandwiches they carried in their snap-tins and ex-Army haversacks. Among the Wincheap drivers' favourite 'caffs' were the Enterprise in Canterbury's Sturry Road (opposite the Vauxhall Tavern); Wheeler's at Barham (next door to Arter's Garage); the Adelaide at Sholden, near Deal; Harry's at Challock; Mrs Gardner's Rose Cabin, on the Ashford road near Milton; and Tommy Dutton's at Charing.

During the school holidays, children whose fathers were lorry drivers, or friends of the drivers, could easily arrange to have a day out in a tipper lorry. Stopping at a transport café was one of the highlights of the outing. Harry's Café is remembered for its delicious meat pies, smothered in brown sauce; at the Adelaide, Christmas lunch with all the trimmings cost 2s 6d, and was enjoyed while watching kingfishers flitting along a nearby stream; at Charing, Tommy Dutton entertained his customers by playing his musical saw. Occasionally when cadging a ride we would load our bikes on to the lorry and ask to be set down out in the country, or at the seaside, so that we could cycle home.

Some of the lorries were not exactly nimble. While hauling a trailer up a hill on the Isle of Grain, BFN 852, a five cylinder ERF, was overtaken by a horse and cart.

The lorry drivers were to be seen at Wincheap Depot at least twice a day, whereas the drivers and operators of Brett Plant Hire Department's mobile plant were less frequent visitors. They did their day's work all over the county, but mechanically-minded youngsters with the right connections had ways and means of wangling their way on to a bulldozer, or into a crane cab. Many a load was shifted with the help of a 14-year-old!

'Top yard' in 1964. Lined up in front of the garage and ready for their next day's work are (from the left) a Commer 7-ton tipper, eight Bedford TKs, a Leyland Super Comet, a Leyland Beaver, a Commer Maxiload and three Commer 7-ton tippers.

George Dilnot (in his cab) and Percy Sackett with their Bedford lorries at 41 St George's Place, Canterbury, *c.* 1951. On the left is the cab of a Brett excavator which is removing rubble during an early phase in the construction of Martin Walter's new garage and showroom. *(Percy Sackett collection)*

Driver Horace Weatherall (centre) with two construction workers at the King's Bridge site on the Isle of Sheppey in August 1958 after delivering a load of clinker from Bowater's Kemsley Mill in AJG 920, an ERF bought new in 1947. *(Nigel Tilly collection)*

From the safety of his cab, Norman Rye observes a spot of bother between Police Sgt Greenham and the owners of some caravans who were resisting eviction from a site in Vauxhall Road, Canterbury, on March 11, 1959. The lorry, DJG 439, had been hired to tow the caravans off the site. It appears to have been resprayed only recently, and its original headboard (seen on page 80) has been replaced. *(Kentish Gazette/ Nigel Tilly collection)*

Norman Rye backs the Leyland Beaver and York low-loader into a corner at 'top yard', soon after the vehicles were delivered in May 1960.

Norman inches his way through Lady Wootton's Green, Canterbury, while hauling a 35-ton 33-RB dragline excavator from Sturry Quarry to a gravel pit in Stodmarsh Road on April 3, 1962. An eight mile detour was made through Canterbury to avoid narrow bridges on the direct route. The man walking behind the load is probably Ernie Allen, manager of Sturry Quarry. *(Kentish Gazette)*

Tom Cavell, operator of Bretts' first wheel-mounted mobile excavator, a Dinkum Digger, at work in Ramsgate's New Castle Hill area, *c.* 1961.

Wincheap Depot's drivers sometimes ran into trouble. Here a Commer lorry is recovered from a ditch in Broad Oak Road, Canterbury, in 1965 by Jim Tunbridge, operating Brett Plant Hire's 11-RB transit crane. *(Charles Bentley collection)*

A Caterpillar D7 hydraulic excavator (left) and a D4 at work with Bedford 6283 FN at the site of Kent and Canterbury Hospital's extension in 1964. *(Charles Bentley collection)*

Another delicate job for the 11-RB's operator. Lifting steelwork in Upper Chantry Lane, Canterbury, in 1966. *(Charles Bentley collection)*

Tony Elvidge, driver of Bedford NJG 445, escaped serious injury when he ran into the River Stour near St Stephen's Road, Canterbury. Wincheap Depot's Bedford QL truck was sent out to recover the lorry. *(Peter Spratt collection)*

The depot also had an ex-Army Scammell Pioneer recovery vehicle, seen here standing by in 'top yard' during a little local difficulty, when a 38-RB crane cab, brought back from one of the quarries for repairs in 1967, slipped off the York trailer while being loaded for its return journey. Central Workshops' manager Bill Knott (far right) is among those dealing with the problem. All this happened in full view of Bretts' head office staff. Afterwards, Jack Martin of Central Workshops told them: 'It's all right for you! You can throw your mistakes into the waste paper basket.' *(Charles Bentley collection)*

The Scammell in School Lane, Blean, in the early 1960s, preparing to recover a bogged-down concrete truckmixer. *(Nigel Tilly)*

A Bedford TK being loaded with gravel by an pneumatically-controlled Ruston-Bucyrus 22-RB ICD crane/dragline (probably operated by Tony White) at Bretts' quarry at Stodmarsh, near Canterbury, in 1967. Wincheap Depot's drivers ran a 'shuttle service' from Stodmarsh to Sturry Quarry's washing and grading plant. Each driver delivered about 22 loads a day.

UJG 663 and another contractor's tractor and trailer in Broad Oak Road, Canterbury, in 1968, hauling two kilns to Bretts' Durite calcined flint plant at Sturry Quarry. The kilns may formerly have been storage tanks at SETAR's tar depot in Broad Oak Road, which closed in 1967. *(Charles Bentley collection)*

Don Rogers' Talbot sports car takes pride of place in this picture taken in 'top yard' in the mid-1960s. The tipper trucks in the background are (left to right) a Leyland Comet (*c.* 1951), a Bedford TK (*c.* 1963), a Commer TS3 (*c.* 1956) and an S-type Bedford (*c.* 1959). *(Charles Bentley collection)*

Les Brice's 'Big Bedford' tipper is loaded with rubble in Canterbury in June 1961 by Wally Twist, operating one of Bretts' 19-RB draglines. The rubble is from the Simon Langton Grammar School, demolished to make way for Riceman's department store.

13: All change at the depot

Brett House and 'top yard' during Robert Brett & Sons' 75th anniversary celebrations. In the foreground are (left to right) AEC Mammoth KJ 5723 (previously seen on page 75), a 1937 Muir Hill loading shovel, a 1905 Wantage traction engine, a 1979 Muir Hill loading shovel and a new Volvo tipper truck. Photographed from the roof of Canterbury Waterworks on June 23, 1979.

IN the mid-1960s Bretts built a new head office — Brett House — on the site of the lorry garage at Wincheap Depot. 'Top yard' became a construction site, the transport fleet was dispersed to temporary parking areas, and for a time Wincheap was denied one of its most familiar sights: impeccably maintained lorries, regimentally ranked in the yard, ready for the next day's work. Brett House opened in September 1966 and Wincheap was once again the company's headquarters, as well as the hub of its haulage and engineering work and social life.

William and Bert Brett had died in 1961 and 1963 respectively but Bretts was still a family firm, headed by Tim Brett and John Brett (William's sons) and Tony Brett, Bert's only surviving son.

The Sixties saw the introduction of new forms of technology that we now take for granted; within a few years, room had to be found at Brett House for the firm's first digital computer.

In 1966 the livery of Bretts' lorries started to undergo a series of changes. The fleet name for the sand and gravel trucks was still 'Bretts Quarries' but they now bore the firm's new logo — a triangle enclosing a pictograph symbolising a gravel stockpile and team effort. Later, the fleet name 'Brett Group' was adopted. In 1987 a simpler logo — the name 'Brett' superimposed on black and yellow stripes — replaced the triangular trademark.

Brett House under construction in 1966, photographed from 'top yard.'
(Charles Bentley collection)

A fine perspective view by Bill Entwistle of Brett House, the works entrance, the precision engineering factory and, in the far distance, Canterbury Cathedral, in June 1967. The five Ford D-series lorries in the foreground date from 1965, when Wincheap Depot's first post-war Fords went into service.

Wincheap Depot and Bretts' Sports Ground in 1967, seen from about the same angle as the aerial picture on page 2. Brett House, completed only a few months earlier, stands on the site of the lorry garage. *(Skyfotos)*

Brett House in mint condition. The lorries are in their new under-cover parking bays; attractive railings and gates have taken the place of the old fences and hoarding around 'top yard;' the flower bed is in bloom; and the Pearce fascia sign spelling out the company's name, originally mounted on the roof of the garage (see page 156) has been erected on the facade.

A 1968 D-series Ford, featuring Brett transport's new livery and the firm's new trademark, negotiates a slippery bend in Fordwich, probably while on the shuttle run from Stodmarsh to Sturry Quarry.

A line-up consisting entirely of Commer lorries in late 1967 or 1968.

New AEC concrete truckmixers at 'top yard' in February 1968, with (left to right) Robin Taylor, John Holman and Frank Macey, Bretts' first truckmixer drivers to become owner drivers. The trucks cost about £4,000 each. Truckmixers were rare visitors to Wincheap Depot. They were based at the company's ready mixed concrete plants and went to Wincheap only for repairs and maintenance, or publicity photocalls.

Learning new office skills. Grouped around their new IBM System 3 Model 6 computer at Brett House in 1973 are (left to right) Sandra Cork, Anne Berry, Chris Godfrey, Ray Castle, Margaret Shaxted (at keyboard), Jo Howard, Flo Howell and Audrey Tindall. To make room for this new technology a computer room was built in the lorry bay next to the main entrance to Brett House.

Jack Ryn delivers sand to the penultimate Channel Tunnel project at Shakespeare Cliff, Dover, in 1975. Ted Tritton (left) and John Douglas inspect progress in the adit. Wincheap Depot's lorries delivered 5,000 tons of sand to this site.

Volvo F86 tipper trucks dating from September 1977 with two ERFs, KJG 64M (right) and GJG 100N, neatly parked in their bays under the offices.

The Volvos, KJG 6M and another mid-1970s ERF, PFN 248M, parked in front of the covered bays. This became the usual arrangement after the computer room was built in the bay behind the ERFs, and a few of the other covered bays were taken over for storage. Since some of the lorries could no longer back into their bays, military precision was maintained by lining them up in front of the office block.

Volvos on parade in 1986: one of the last pictures of the fleet before its livery was changed.

A Volvo tipper truck and a Leyland Constructor/Liebherr truckmixer in 'top yard' in 1987, featuring Bretts' new livery and logo.

Volvos and Scanias bearing the livery currently in use.

Not always immaculate! Driver Bob Sandy escaped serious injury when the body of his Leyland lorry self-tipped and became wedged under a bridge on the M2 in 1989.

Brian Amos backs his 1990 Scania P93ML 8x4R 280 lorry into a loading bay at Milton Quarry, near Canterbury. Brian and three other Wincheap-based owner drivers working under contract to Bretts bought the first Scanias to trade in Brett livery.

Keith Cork applies the Brett logo to a Scania 113MA 6x2 360 hp tractor in 'top yard' in 1995. This was one of the last HGVs to be delivered to Wincheap Depot.

14: A skilled team

Left to right: Vic Symonds, Lance Betts, Bill Terry, Malcolm Brown, David Wing and Bert Luckhurst of Canterbury Precision Engineers in 'bottom yard' in October 1979, with a crawler-mounted drilling rig built for open-cast coal mining exploration in Scotland. *(Kentish Gazette/Frank Terry collection)*

FOR more than one hundred years Wincheap Depot was the workplace of some of the Canterbury area's most skilled engineers, mechanics and craftsmen. A main repair shop for road vehicles, mobile plant and demountable heavy machinery, and workshops for carpenters, electricians, metal fabricators, painters and welders, were located around 'bottom yard' and there was a tyre fitting shop near the lorry parking bays in 'top yard.'

Most of these departments were part of Central Workshops, whose main job was to look after Bretts' lorries and plant. In 1959, when the firm set up a ready mixed concrete company, servicing truckmixers and batching plant added still more variety to Central Workshops' duties.

Occasionally, the team faced the challenge of restoring some of Bretts' historic vehicles. They gave KJ 5723, the 1932 AEC Mammoth lorry, an external refurbishment for the company's 75th anniversary display, and helped Stephen and Hugh Brett restore Aveling & Porter road roller 11055, the sole survivor from Bretts' steam fleet, which had been out of service since the 1950s. Later, the workshops' carpenters restored a house van in which traction engine crews slept overnight when away from home. Originally it was probably one of Robert Brett's horse-drawn furniture removal vans. In 1991, William Brett's 1937 Humber was restored, to take Bill Brett (one of William and Florence Brett's grandsons) and his bride Rachel to their wedding. A generation earlier the car, driven by Tom Sackett, the company's chauffeur, had been on similar duty when William and Florence's sons and daughters were married.

Central Workshops' neighbour, Canterbury Precision Engineers Ltd, produced high-quality work for the aircraft industry and made a fascinating variety of other products including butter moulds, conveyors, hydraulic drilling rigs and potato crisp packaging equipment.

Bill Knott attends to one of Bretts' motor cars in 'bottom yard', c. 1935. Chauffeur Tom Sackett keeps him company. *(Colin Smith collection)*

Bert Andrews (at the third machine from the right), Sid Holden (glimpsed through the drive belts in the foreground) and other operators at work in the machine shop, *c.* 1950. Below: Bert Andrews operating a Landis machine tool, *c.* 1950. *(Jack Martin collection)*

George Fassum (left) and John Wyborn in the paint shop, respraying an ex-Army Albion or Thornycroft lorry, *c.* 1946.

Jimmy Hacker (foreground) and (left to right) Sid Smith, Ron Collins, John Wyborn and Ron Feakins, rebuilding lorry bodies *c.* 1950. *(Jack Martin collection)*

The transport workshop in February 1982. Various vans, a Volvo tipper truck and two Leyland truckmixers are in for repair. Peter Spratt's mobile workshop, a Luton-bodied Ford Transit van, is parked in the far left corner. *(George Weatherall)*

Aveling & Porter steam roller 11055 (previously seen on page 52) in 'bottom yard' in 1985, with restorers Lance Betts and Keith Cork (on footplate) and (left to right) Stephen Brett, Hugh Brett and Tony Brett. After many years' service on road repair contracts, the roller worked at Bretts' quarries until the 1950s.

AEC Mammoth KJ 5723 in 'bottom yard' in April 1982, by when it was 50 years old. *(George Weatherall)*

Workshops manager Jack Martin (right) and fitter Jim Troup, retiring after 41½ and 18 years' service respectively, at their retirement party in 1989 with Tony Brett and colleagues. Photographed in Central Workshops' paint shop, near the entrance to the carpenters' shop.

John Hatch, who joined Bretts as an apprentice fitter in 1950, photographed in Central Workshops in 1990.

Carpenters Roy Trice and Ron Feakins (on ladder), restoring the house van, built *c.* 1920, in 1990.

Derek Friend, plant and transport fitter, in 1990. Derek worked for Elgar Brett & Sons in Gordon Road, Wincheap, in the 1950s and for Robert Brett & Sons for more than 30 years.

Michael Knight working on the 1937 Humber in 1990.

15: Wincheap veterans

Retired employees ready to set off from 'top yard' on an outing to Windsor in 1984. Wincheap was the departure point for many Brett outings. Before boarding their coaches the pensioners found time to say 'hello' to former colleagues in the offices; and the directors came down to the yard to wish the pensioners an enjoyable day. *(Kentish Gazette)*

VETERAN employees based at Wincheap and Bretts' other departments were always fêted at important stages in their lives. The retirement of a popular colleague after many years' service was marked by an informal presentation of farewell gifts. Employees who achieved 25 years' continuous service received a gold watch or carriage clock from the board of directors, and there were special awards to employees after 40 or more years. The first long-service ceremony was held during the 50th anniversary dinner in 1954; the next one took place on March 17, 1962, at an employees' dinner at Canterbury's County Hotel. This was the occasion at which the Brett 25 Club was formed for those who had been with the firm for 25 years or more. The club meets every two years at a dinner at which the latest veterans receive their awards.

Two men set unusual employment records. In January 1992 carpenter Ron

Feakins completed 50 years' service at Wincheap Depot and four months later became Robert Brett & Sons' longest serving full-time employee. He retired in October 1992. Ron joined Bretts ten weeks after his fourteenth birthday and belonged to the last generation able to work for 50 years before reaching retirement age. In 1993, at the age of 80, retired chauffeur Tom Sackett set an even more remarkable record of 65 years' service: 49½ full-time, 15½ as part-time caretaker of 'top yard' and 'bottom yard.'

As this book went to press, two veterans would soon become the first Brett employees to complete 25 years of retirement: Charles Bentley, who worked at Wincheap for 17 of his 45 years with the company; and Percy Blunt, who was a Foden engineman and driver at Wincheap during his early years with the firm.

In 1974, annual summer outings for pensioners and their spouses were introduced. The destination for the first trip was a watersports centre at Lydd, created on lakes at one of Bretts' restored quarries.

The retirement parties, long-service awards, 25 Club dinners and summer outings ensured that pensioners and veteran employees continued to meet regularly. These events, always an opportunity to reminisce about 'the old days' at Wincheap, continue to this day and are part of Brett life.

Employees from Wincheap Depot and other Brett departments at the long service celebration dinner in 1962, after receiving gold watches for 25 or more years' service. In the picture with Bert, Tony, Tim and John Brett and Jack Snell, general manager, are recipients George Beer, Jim Clarke, George Dilnot, John Hoddinott, Bill Horne, Vernon Kirby, Bill Longley, Ian Newing, Percy Sackett, Richard Skelton, Ken Todd, Doug Toze, Horace Weatherall, Jack Young and Ken Young.

Several men who were colleagues on the cricket field as well as at work are in this group at the 1962 dinner. Left to right: Alan Shaxted, Ernest Bradshaw, Fred Tritton, Ian Newing (standing), Tony Haydon and Fred Austen.

On another table, five other Wincheap workmates shelter behind a cluster of beer glasses and bottles. Left to right: George Fassum, Jim Tunbridge, Bert Killian, Mick Fry (standing) and Sid Smith.

The Brett 25 Club dinner on April 8, 1965. Left to right (top table): (1) Tim Brett, (2) Winifred Smith, (3) Jack Kinnear; back row: (1) Bill Knott, (2) Jack Young, (3) John Ratcliff, (4) Norman Rye, (5) Harry Rye, (6) Ted Tritton; second row: (1) Sid Burton, (2) Wally Twist, (3) Ken Todd, (4) Albert Ades, (5) George Beer, (6) B. Bubb; third row: (1) Horace Weatherall, (2) Harry Ward, (3) Cliff Miles, (4) Bill Gipps, (5) Fred Marsh; fourth row: (1) Fred Tritton, (2) Mick Fry, (3) Fred Jones, (4) Jim Hawkins, (5) Tom Hatch; row nearest camera: (1) George Dilnot, (2) Arthur Hammond, (3) Ernie Allen, (4) Ken Young. *(Kentish Gazette)*

Brett directors with employees who received long service awards at the Brett 25 Club dinner in November 1974: Left to right: (1) Tim Brett, (2) Les Kayes, (3) Ted Tritton, (4) Sid Burton, (5) Ken Cox, (6) Tony Brett, (7) Tom Sackett, (8) John Brett, (9) Harry Rye, (10) Albert Ades, (11) Bert Sackett. *(Kentish Gazette)* **Foot of opposite page: Brett directors and managers with employees from Wincheap Depot and other departments who received long service awards at the Brett 25 Club dinner on December 7, 1972. Left to right, standing on floor: (1) Tim Brett, (2) John Brett, (3) Tony Brett, (4) D. Smith (collecting the award for which his father, Sidney C. Smith, qualified a few months before he died), (5) Bert Killian, (6) Cyril West, (7) Jack Snell (general manager), (8) Jack Martin, (9) Jim Hacker; standing on platform: (1) Arthur Stokes, (2) George West, (3) Edward Stokes, (4) George Weatherall, (5) George Webster, (6) Ernest Hogben, (7) Horace Friend.** *(Kentish Gazette)*

Wincheap colleagues Don Laraman, Don Martin and Audrey Tindall (first, second and fifth from left) with Geoff Clarke, Tim Brett and Ted Scott at the long service awards presentation in 1976. *(Kentish Gazette)*

Retired employees assemble in 'top yard' in 1979 for their annual outing. Their destination was Chiddingstone Castle. *(Kentish Gazette)*

Members and guests at the Brett 25 Club dinner at the Chiesman Pavilion, St Lawrence Cricket Ground, Canterbury, in 1982. *(Kentish Gazette)*

Rita Wilson (foreground) with colleagues from Wincheap and other departments who received long service awards at the 1986 Brett 25 Club dinner. Tony Brett (left) and Tim Brett (behind Rita) joined the photocall. Rita has organised all the Brett 25 Club dinners since 1965, and all the pensioners' outings. *(Kentish Gazette)*

Wincheap colleagues Reg Smith, Colin Smith, Roy Kemp, Alan Mynheer and Beryl Clayson (first, fourth, sixth, seventh and eighth from left), Peter Goodsell and Tom Cavell check their new timepieces against an antique clock during the Brett 25 Club dinner at the County Hotel, Canterbury, in 1984. With them are Tony Brett and Tim Brett.

Tom Sackett is presented with a special gift — a barograph — by Tim Brett in 1993 to commemorate his 65 years' service at Wincheap Depot.

Ron Feakins receives a commemorative certificate in May 1992 after becoming Bretts' longest serving full-time employee. Company chairman Tim Brett makes the presentation, watched by Brett directors Peter Woolnough, Stephen Brett, John Peer and Tony Brett. *(Kentish Gazette)*

Dennis Owen (second from left), who worked at Brett House from the day it opened, with Bretts' bell-ringing team at St Nicholas' Church, Thanington, on December 22, 1995. The team dedicated its traditional Christmas quarter-peal to Dennis, who retired a few months later after nearly 35 years with the firm. With Dennis are (from the left) Chris Godfrey and Nigel Miller from Brett House, and Phil Harding, Janet Godfrey and Keith Osborne. Chris became a member of the Brett 25 Club in 1994; Nigel, who also worked at Brett House from the day it opened to the day it closed, received his award for 25 years' service in 1986.

Retired driver Percy Blunt, with his picture of himself and the road repair gang at Knaves Ash, Hoath, in 1930 (see page 50).

Charles and Dora Bentley at Brett House in September 1995 with (standing, left to right) Tony Brett, Winifred Newing, Margaret Brett, Tim Brett, Ken Cox, Stephen Brett, Ian Newing, Jenny Brett, Rita Wilson and Joan Cox. Charles and Dora are admiring his 90th birthday present from Bretts — an album of photographic memories of his 45 years with the company.

16: Goodbye, Wincheap

Reg Beasley, who worked at Bretts' offices in Wincheap for 24 years, with his painting of colleagues practising bat and trap on the sports ground in 1983. Reg painted the scene after revisiting the sports ground in 1994 and based it on a sketch he made shortly before he retired.

WHEN Bretts started to open new branches and businesses both within and beyond east Kent in the 1980s, and to set up separate headquarters for its various divisions, the redevelopment of the Wincheap site became inevitable. Most of Brett House's staff moved to new locations, leaving behind departments that could easily be accommodated in a much smaller building. The opening of the Canterbury by-pass in 1981 enhanced the value of the site, since it was only a minute's drive from sliproads giving direct access to the A2. The closure of Canterbury Precision Engineers Ltd in 1985 and Central Workshops in 1992 further reduced the number of people employed at Wincheap, and released more land for redevelopment.

In 1982 Canterbury City Council published proposals to extend the Wincheap Industrial Estate on to the sports ground and Thanington Allotment Gardens. Various other schemes were put forward, the final outcome being a Park and Ride terminus on the allotments and a superstore and group of retail units on Bretts' land. The lane that formerly led to the sports ground and pavilion became the main access to the new development and was named Ten Perch Road, a unit of measurement familiar to allotment holders.

In the years leading up to redevelopment, many retired employees went to Wincheap to say goodbye to the place where they had worked and enjoyed sports and social events for so many years. A photographic record was made of the site, and Bretts put its collection of historic vehicles and artifacts into storage, for eventual display in the museum the company hopes to create at its new group headquarters at Milton Manor Farm — an estate with a longer and even more interesting history than the Wincheap site.

Brett lorries were last seen lined-up in 'top yard' on the morning of February 7, 1996. When the drivers finished their day's work they drove to their new depot at Milton Manor Farm. Moving-out operations from the offices began on Friday, March 1, continued throughout the weekend, and were completed by March 4. Brett House and 'top yard' were handed over to Safeway Stores on March 14 and the final phase of the redevelopment of the site — the construction of six 'retail units' — began.

The Brett group's new HQ is set amid parkland and meadows beside the River Stour, and has been created around a 17th century barn which has been restored and converted into offices for Bretts' main board directors, senior managers and their staff. The building has been named 'Robert Brett House', in memory of the firm's founder, whose family still owns the firm.

The Canterbury by-pass under construction in 1979. Wincheap Depot and Brett House are on the left. Drastic remodelling of the junction of Wincheap, Thanington Road and Cockering Road is taking place. *(Kentish Gazette)*
Opposite page: Brett House and the junction of Wincheap Street, Thanington Road and Cockering Road in November 1973, when various options for the Canterbury by-pass were announced. G.F. Finn's traction engine halted here about 80 years earlier for the photograph on page 24. *(Kentish Gazette)*

Constructing a temporary diversion road on the A28 in the summer of 1980 for traffic approaching and leaving Canterbury while the Thanington Road bridge over the by-pass was being built. Brett House is on the left.

An unusually quiet moment on the A28 approach to Wincheap on a summer evening in 1995, viewed from almost the same position as the previous photograph. Lamp posts, signals, signs and barriers have replaced the trees in the picture on page 194.

Leyland truckmixers, a ballast lorry and a Muir Hill loading shovel in 'the orchard', the parking compound near 'bottom yard, in April 1982. *(George Weatherall)*

Wincheap Depot in 1987. Brett House is at the top of the picture; Canterbury Waterworks, Wincheap Street, Lillywhite's oast house and outbuildings behind the Hop Poles pub fill the top left-hand corner. In the foreground are the First World War aeroplane hangar, 'bottom yard' and (under the striped roof) the lorry brake testing pits. The building with the pitched roofs in the middle distance was constructed in several phases. The first and second bays from the left originally housed Central Workshops. The lorry repair shop's inspection pits were immediately inside the first door; the second door led into the paint shop. In or soon after 1942 both bays were converted into a munitions factory and the workshops were moved to a new building constructed alongside the sports ground. This is the long, white building, with side and end doors, which is very prominent in the picture on page 2. In the 1950s a fourth bay was built in the space between the original bays and the new building: the entrance to bay 4 can be seen immediately in front of the tipper truck. Until 1985 most of bays 1, 2 and 4 were occupied by the precision engineering works.

The sports pavilion, flanked by Bretts' canteen and (far end) technical laboratory, seen from Brett House on April 13, 1994, shortly before the buildings were demolished. The Wincheap 'Park and Ride' car park is being built between the pavilion and the Canterbury by-pass, on the site of Thanington Allotment Gardens.

The same location on October 1, 1994, when the Wincheap 'Park and Ride' Service opened.

Salvaged when the pavilion was demolished: the pavilion's foundation stone and the stone unveiled by Les Ames when the extension was opened in 1976.

The first of three views of Wincheap Depot's 'carpenters' yard' in 1990. This is where Robert Brett set up his business in the early years of this century. Retired chauffeur Tom Sackett is standing outside the mess room where enginemen working for G.F. Finn, Robert Brett & Sons and other haulage contractors obtained basic bed-and-breakfast accommodation when their work kept them away from home overnight. The side wall of No. 4 Thanington Cottages, Robert's home until 1908, is on the left. Tom, who died in 1993, lived in the cottage with his wife Barbara for more than 40 years.

The steam engine repair shop, which later became Wincheap Depot's second carpenters' shop. The first one was next door to the mess room.

This shed was the depot's office in the early years of Robert Brett & Sons. While demolishing the shed a year after this picture was taken, Keith Cork of Central Workshops found two metal spikes in the roof space. Fixed to them were several hundred bills, receipts and other documents dating back to 1909. Remarkably intact after being concealed for some 80 years, they have yielded historical details about Robert Brett's business which could easily have been lost for ever.

A partly dismantled terrace at Bretts' Corner on June 6, 1994, looking towards the grandstand. Shoots sprout from the roots of Robert Brett's poplar tree (centre, foreground), planted in 1935. The tree grew through the roof of the terrace but after flourishing for 52 years it was blown down by the hurricane that felled many trees in Canterbury in October 1987.

Now concealed by trees, the grandstand at Bretts' Corner on June 6, 1994, viewed from where the incident on page 135 was photographed in 1972.

Wincheap Depot drivers Bob Cooper (third from left), Fred Hogben (4), Jack Ryn (6), Tom Chapman (7), Don Martin (8), Ken Hawkins (9) and Albert Furner (10) at 'top yard'. With them are Tim Marsh, John Matthews and Nigel Miller of Bretts' transport department. The picture was taken in July 1991 when Jack retired after 39 years as a tar tanker and tipper truck driver.

Staff of Brett House in 'top yard' on January 24, 1996, a few weeks before they moved to their new offices.

Wincheap and more distant parts of Canterbury, viewed from Brett House on February 29, 1996. This panorama rewarded those who were prepared to climb a vertical ladder into the plant room, and from there venture on to the roof. On the left, construction work progresses on the site of the precision engineering factory and Central Workshops, and the eye is drawn to Canterbury Cathedral on the skyline. The prominent buildings on the right are Lillywhite's oast house (now owned by Bretts) and the block of flats in Woodville Close.

This view from Brett House, also taken on February 29, 1996, shows the Safeway superstore taking shape on the site of the sports field. The Wincheap gasometer (previously seen on page 21) and the industrial estate off Cow Lane are on the right. Beyond the construction site, a London-bound train crosses the bridge over the River Stour and the water tower on St Thomas' Hill reflects the winter sunshine.

A Pickfords removal van passes Brett House and heads for the Brett group's new HQ at Milton Manor Farm. As staff finished their last day's work at Brett House on March 1, 1996, a fleet of pantechnicons moved into 'top yard.' Over the next 48 hours, 17 vanloads of office furniture and equipment were removed, either to Milton Manor Farm or to Bysing Wood, Faversham, where the company opened a new headquarters for its sand and gravel division.

Tim Brett (fourth from left), chairman of Robert Brett & Sons Ltd, locks the gates to 'top yard' for the last time, as the Brett family firm's links with Wincheap came to an end in March, 1996, after 112 years. With Tim are his fellow directors Stephen Brett, John Peer, Bill Brett, Tony Brett and Peter Woolnough.

17: In Robert's footsteps

Thanington Cottages, Wincheap. Robert Brett and his family lived at No. 4 (nearest camera) until 1908 and then moved three doors down the street to Prospect House. 'Carpenters' yard' is behind the brick wall; the blocked-up windows to the carpenters' shop (left) and the enginemen's mess room can still be seen. Photographed in April 1994.

REMINDERS of the days when George Felix Finn and Robert Brett lived and worked in Wincheap can still be found. Thanington Cottages and Marlowe Terrace survive, as does 'carpenters' yard', which was not part of the site sold to Safeway for redevelopment in 1995.

No. 4 Thanington Cottages, which became 99 Wincheap when the street was first renumbered, is now No. 274 Wincheap. Prospect House, formerly No.96 and now No. 268, has a new name — Wincheap Grange. Culham, five doors down the street and once the home of Bert and Winifred Brett and their family, is now a guest-house called Carena.

On the rare occasions when the gate to 'carpenters' yard' is open, a few disused workshops can be seen within, including two lean-to buildings supported by the brick wall that runs alongside the pavement in Wincheap. One of these buildings stands on the site of the depot's first carpenters' shop (which was destroyed in a fire), the other was the steam enginemen's mess room. The two blocked-up openings in the wall were once windows into these buildings.

Traction engines were overhauled in the yard, either in the open or under a tarpaulin. When major surgery was necessary they were driven into the engine workshop a few yards away. Intimate inspections of their nether regions were made from an inspection pit just inside the workshop door. Broken wheels and other fractured parts were trundled into the forge next door. The forge was demolished several years ago but the engine shop, which became the depot's second carpenters' shop in about 1920, survives. Workmen could walk from these buildings into 'bottom yard' but 'carpenters' yard' was really a world of its own, set apart from the hurly-burly of the rest of the depot.

Beside the gate into the yard there is another blocked-up aperture in the wall. This was a hatch for a pipeline from a hand-operated pump which stood just inside the gate. Lorries requiring fuel would pull up in the street, 'toot' to alert the depot's pump attendant, and top-up without having to drive into the yard. In earlier days employees queued at the hatch to receive their week's wages.

The Hop Poles, at the other end of Marlowe Terrace, is still the first and last pub in Wincheap, and although the dairy and Waterworks Cottages were demolished long ago, Lillywhite's oast house remains, now owned by Robert Brett & Sons and occupied by 'Pine & Things.'

Past the site of Brett House, Ten Perch Road follows the alignment of the lane that led to the County Athletic Grounds and Bretts' Corner and takes us to the Park & Ride and Safeways. Standing here today it is, admittedly, difficult to see signs of bygone days and imagine things as they were. To jog the memory, look back towards Wincheap Street, for glimpses of the rooftops that were part of the backcloth to many pictures of the arena on which so many exciting and spectacular events were staged.

No. 1 Marlowe Terrace (left), once the home of George Felix Finn and his family; the gates to 'carpenter's yard;' and (beside the lamp post) the hatch through which wages and motor fuel were dispensed. Photographed in April 1994.

The Hop Poles and part of Marlowe Terrace. Although many changes have occurred at this end of Wincheap since the picture on page 33 was taken, the pub and the terrace are substantially unaltered. Photographed on October 1, 1994.

Demolition of Central Workshops and other buildings on the south-east boundary of the sports ground in the autumn of 1995 revealed this long-concealed view of several properties in Wincheap Street, including (from right to left) Lillywhite's oast house, the Hop Poles pub, Marlowe Terrace and Thanington Cottages. Their roofs and chimneys were previously seen through gaps in the trees in the views on pages 11 and 19 — 23. This picture was taken on February 29, 1996, from about the same position, while roads and parking areas for the new superstore and retail units were being constructed. What would the owner of the early motor car in the picture on page 23 make of the cars seen here today?

Aveling & Porter road roller no. 11055, the sole survivor from Robert Brett's steam transport fleet, passes Thanington Cottages, Wincheap, on March 8, 1996, on the last journey from Wincheap Depot by a steam road locomotive. With steam engineer Martin Staniforth as driver, Stephen Brett as steersman and Phil Harding as relief steersman, 11055 travelled from Canterbury to Stelling Minnis via Hollow Lane, Street End and Upper Hardres, following country roads familiar to Robert in the days when he drove Aveling & Porter traction engines to collect 'surface picked flints' from farms on the North Downs. The 72-year-old engine proceeded at a leisurely six miles an hour, consuming 3 cwt of coal and 80 gallons of water during the six mile journey.